Sneha!

EVERYONE'S IN SALES

Stop Apologizing!

All the Bsst.

2016

Testimonials

Nothing rings truer for me today than Todd Cohen's mantra, *Everyone's In Sales*. And yet I continue to see most leaders try to insulate and isolate themselves from the "sales function" and its service mandate, seemingly oblivious to the truth that sales and service constitute the essence of the enterprise. If you want to create a sales culture where more sales happen, I suggest you work with Todd Cohen.

—K.S., Editor and CEO, Leadership Excellence

Todd is an absolutely amazing motivator and speaker. In my 16+ years of sales positions, I have been to and heard many, many speakers attempt to motivate and claim they can produce more sales. Todd Cohen is the ONLY professional that has actually made that come true!

I hired Todd to speak to my team of senior sales professionals, and the results they produced after incorporating his "Everyone's in Sales" methodology were astounding. They were so motivated and ready to take their jobs to the next level it was phenomenal.

There is no question I will be working with Todd continuously to boost my team's performances in the future. Your return on investment will be like nothing you have ever seen in the past—trust me!"

—B.S., SVP Sales and Marketing, CARCO Inc.

Todd has an innate ability to to connect the concepts and principles of sales and business development to people to people who don't always see themselves in that role.

—C.B., Office Managing Partner, EY

Todd is dynamic, engaging and compelling! His Sales Culture message removes any of the fear or negative connotations associated with the word "sales" . . . we ALL do it!

—S.S., Vice President, NFL Players, Inc.

Todd is a masterful public speaker with unparalled expertise in building sales culture in organizations. Easily commanding a room while authentically engaging his audience, Todd leads organizations on journeys to new heights of actionable sales knowledge resulting in optimal team-selling effectiveness. Todd utilizes fundamental selling tenets, his own unique insights, and memorable examples, all presented in riveting fashion with generous dollops of coaching and humor to successfully impart his message with his audience. Any organization looking to leverage other parts of the company to maximize their selling effectiveness should talk with Todd.

—M.S., Director of Sales Operations, Vertex, Inc.

Over the years I have heard many speakers and those who claim to be speakers and I can say that Todd Cohen is the real deal. His topic of building a sales culture is timely, unique and in a class by itself. Todd's speaking style is amazing—he is very engaging and Todd works and keeps the room's attention throughout his keynotes! He blends the right amount humility, vulnerability, storytelling and practicality in one motivating and inspiring package. I would strongly suggest booking Todd for your next gathering.

—M.J.H., Adjunct Professor and Small Business Advisor

I saw Todd Cohen speak at a recent conference and was blown away. His easy going style and command of the room kept the participants awake, alive, laughing, learning and most importantly. . . . ready to sell! I highly recommend Todd for any group of business people who are looking to increase their sales. Which means everyone.

—G.M., Speaker, Author, National Business Columnist & Business Owner, The Marks Group

I strongly recommend Todd Cohen as an individual any organization wanting to increase results more broadly than just through the sales channel should engage. I engaged Todd on behalf of CDI IT Solutions to assist in developing a sales culture across the organization and found value in every recommendation. Additionally, by using him personally to assist with implementation, we accelerated our becoming an industry leader and outpaced our competitors.

Driving the desired culture requires numerous initiatives and tremendous motivation. Todd is an exceptional motivational speaker with an ability to resonate across the organization from sales to accounting to human resources. As yet another value added benefit of engaging Todd, he was able to provide one-on-one coaching to selected individuals to both drive results and improve our management depth.

Delivery of bottom line results is a prerequisite for any successful senior leader; however, given the difficult economic times, companies and leadership all too often fall into defensive posturing—attempting to preserve and protect rather than to challenge the organization, attack the competition and seek to grow, even in difficult times. Todd Cohen can assist in harnessing the entire organization to drive the top line, improve margins and increase productivity. . . . all by creating an appropriate sales culture throughout.

—A.C., CEO, SDI, Inc.

Todd Cohen is 'one-of-a-kind'! He is an exceptional speaker . . . informative, inclusive and high-energy. Most important is that his message has long-lasting value. This is what differentiates Todd from the pack of choices you have in exposing your sales team to new thinking. His message is impactful . . . challenging . . . and it stays with you. He is smart, professional, likable and proactive in giving to others. Check him out!

—J.M., Senior Leadership, ECRI

Todd Cohen is captivating audiences all over the country. He delivers a powerful keynote speech with conviction and humor. He is America's expert on "Sales Culture" and his strategies will take your company's "Sales" to a new level. If you want your profits to soar and your people to produce give him a call today.

—C.R., President, Grow Ur Biz and Carol Talks

Todd presented his signature topic of "Sales Culture" to our Society for Information Managers NJ chapter. The topic, presentation, energy and content was an absolutely excellent way for NJ SIM to start our calendar year.

—B.J., SIM Director

Todd Cohen is an exceptional speaker. I heard Todd keynote about sales culture and the entire audience was moved, inspired and having fun! Todd is engaging and interactive and makes his points in a clear and concise way. He would make an excellent addition to any meeting.

—T.B., V. President—Sales and Services, Promotion

EVERYONE'S IN SALES

Stop Apologizing!

How to Get What You NEED, WANT and DESERVE

Todd Cohen

KEYNOTE SPEAKER, TRAINER AND AUTHOR

SalesLeader, LLC

Philadelphia, Pennsylvania

Everyone's in Sales—Stop Apologizing!
How to Get What You Need, Want and Deserve

Published by
Sales Culture Press LLC
Philadelphia, Pennsylvania
866-515-9445

Photos on pages 10 and 26 are copyright Annmarie Young Photography and are used by permission.

Photos on page 97 and 105 are credited to Torre Studios

ISBN: 978-0-9828722-6-0 (hardcover)
ISBN: 978-0-9828722-7-7 (softcover)
ISBN: 978-0-9828722-8-4 (Kindle)
ISBN: 978-0-9828722-9-1 (eBook)

Cover and Interior Design and Typesetting:
Desktop Miracles, Inc., Stowe, VT

For information contact:
Todd Cohen
Sales Leader LLC
www.toddcohen.com

When I wrote my first book, Everyone's in Sales, *I dedicated it to the memory of my father because so much of what I speak and write about I had learned from him.*

This book is all about what I have learned from my clients, colleagues, and friends who have supported me every step of the way in my journey as a speaker and an author. I wish I could name everyone, but the list would be longer than the book.

With deep gratitude and appreciation for believing in me and for giving me an opportunity, I dedicate this book to each of you.

Contents

Author's Note

Many things got me excited about writing this book. What excited me most was the challenge of making *Everyone's in Sales—Stop Apologizing!* different from a "typical" business book.

There are many great business books on the market, and I'm not trying to knock them. I've read these books and they've helped me tremendously in my career. They are intelligent. They are well written. They are full of great ideas and valuable insight and practical advice and solid analysis.

To me though, these books often seem written for professional business people: men and women who studied business in school and who are managers and executives or owners of companies.

I wanted to write a book that would speak to—and help— everyone from the C Suite to the reception desk, from seasoned entrepreneurs to people taking their first steps toward inventing or reinventing their work lives. I wanted to speak to everyone because I believe everyone needs to sell themselves well to succeed in today's world.

Because I wanted to speak to everyone, this book is first and foremost a primer on the attitudes and actions we need in order to sell effectively. I have assumed that my readers are brand-new to selling, even though I know many of them are not.

If you are an experienced business person or sales professional, my hope is you will find here some useful reminders of things you already know. If you are new to selling, I want to make you ready to go sell yourself when you are done reading this book!

Because the emotions and energy we project are important to selling ourselves, I've included chapters that might have a "self-help" feel to some readers. I'm not a self-help guru and am not trying to become one. However, qualities like passion and confidence are as essential to selling as they are unusual to discuss in a business book. As someone who is primarily a keynote speaker on selling and Sales Culture, I hope that I've discussed these qualities in the right way.

I wanted to make reading this book feel as if we were talking over a cup of coffee, so I wrote the way I speak. This means that some of my sentences might be marked by my high school English teachers with red pencils. I hope you'll see accepting my occasionally less than strictly grammatical constructions as a fair trade for a lively conversation.

Finally, I hope you find something of use to you in this book. If there is just one thing here that helps you get what you need, want, and deserve, I will be grateful and delighted.

Wishing you the best of all success!

TODD COHEN
Philadelphia, Pennsylvania
Fall 2014

Foreword

When Todd Cohen asked me to read the manuscript for *Everyone's in Sales—Stop Apologizing!*, I was happy to agree for two reasons. First, Todd's conviction we are all in sales matches deeply my experiences as an entrepreneur. Second, his idea of the "Sales Apologist" reminded me of a statement I had made early in my career: "I would never want to be in sales."

These words haunted me as I stood in front a group of investors one time, working to convince them that my startup business was worthy of their time and money. Selling them that I had a viable idea and business model was going to be the difference between success and failure for me and my team. As an entrepreneur and CEO, I was the most important sales person in the company.

Entrepreneurs usually define themselves by their backgrounds, by their skills, or by their industry. We don't always call entrepreneurs sales people, and entrepreneurs don't always think of themselves as sales people because of that. Further, the people entrepreneurs hire, such as programmers, creatives, and program managers, define themselves by the fantastic skills they've developed over the years. We rarely ever call these professionals sales people, and most of them don't see selling as part of their job.

Yet as an entrepreneur, I am always selling. I am selling in order to build a team. I am selling to get investment. I am selling to develop press relations. And of course I am selling in order to get my first customers.

It's not just the CEO and the founding team that need to be in sales, however. As an extension of the CEO, every single person in a startup company has to contribute to the sales efforts. It doesn't matter if you're the technical developer, you need to be in sales. It doesn't matter if you're the most creative person on the team, you need to be in sales. As part of the core startup team, you are selling the world every day on the idea of the business and the potential of the value proposition. Everything is new, and the survival of the business and your career are at stake.

Entrepreneurs and their teams need to do many things right in order to be successful. Probably sales is the most important thing all of them need to do. I admit, I'm in sales, and it's the only thing that's actually going to make my startup company matter.

I believe those lessons apply to everybody, not just people like me who have started businesses, and that's another reason I liked *Everyone's in Sales—Stop Apologizing!* Todd Cohen really has written a sales book that speaks to everyone. For someone like me, this book is an engaging reminder of the fundamentals I need to practice every day. For new-comers to selling or anyone getting started in business (like many of the students at my institution), it is an energetic and effective introduction to selling and more importantly, the mind-sets and behaviors that lead to professional success.

CHUCK SACCO
Entrepreneur in Residence and Director of
External Relations for The Charles D. Close School of
Entrepreneurship, Drexel University

Introduction:

Selling Is the Common Thread of Our Success

When I was growing up, my father and my mother and my favorite aunt used to say "if you are good at math and reading, you will be successful." They told me "reading and math are the common threads to success."

I listened to them and became a voracious reader and pretty decent at math, although I have never figured out the practical applications of geometry. When I became an adult and began my career in sales, however, I realized there was one more common thread to success.

This common thread—the behavior that separates the good from the great and the successful from the mediocre—is the ability to show how our work helps make other people's lives better. This common thread is our ability to sell ourselves and to sell without apologizing!

I have made my career showing how everyone's in sales. This isn't a new idea, and I don't see myself as a trendsetter for talking about it. I just see the words "everyone's in sales" as an overdue reinforcement of *reality.*

It is astonishing (and frightening) how soon we become complacent in a new job or business opportunity. We forget to keep selling and we lose our edge. You *know* I'm right. It's so easy to think "everyone knows what I do" when the fact is not everybody does. Every interaction we have is an opportunity to influence and build relationships with people who can help us.

I recently met with a colleague who offered to make some introductions for me. Ironically, one person he introduced me to was someone I had met a few years earlier when he was in transition. Today, this person is in a good job. His reaction to the proposed introduction? "Please don't bother me with people trying to market themselves." Needless to say both my colleague and I were shocked. This man forgot that just a few years earlier, he was trying to market himself.

I never forget that we all have to market ourselves—to sell ourselves every day. These are the reasons I wrote this book. To convince you selling is the common thread to success and to give you the tools to make selling easy. Let's begin right now!

1

Selling Is the Common Thread to Getting What We Need, Want and Deserve

Salesmanship is limitless. Our very living is selling. We are all salespeople.

—James Cash Penney

My mission in this book is to help you get what you need and want, and to enjoy the life you deserve!

We're going to do this by talking about selling and how to sell ourselves well. We're going to talk about selling in many different ways and have fun doing it.

We'll meet the "Sales Apologist"—that voice in our heads that says we should apologize, should feel embarrassed or guilty, whenever we sell. We are going to kick our Sales Apologists out of our heads and feel great when we sell.

Then we'll talk about how to use simple, powerful selling techniques. The most important things to know about these techniques are that you can *feel good* about them and that you are *already doing many of them*. We don't need to do anything differently to sell. We just need to think differently about what we do. I say that all the time in my keynotes and workshops, and I love the chance to say it again here.

Finally, we're going to talk about what you need, want, and deserve—those things you want to get by selling. Practical "next step" exercises at the end of each chapter will help you develop the knowledge and skills to get what you want.

There are several reasons why selling is the common thread to success. First, how we sell ourselves—our skills, our knowledge, our experience, our energy, our drive, our desire, our focus, our value—determines whether we get what we want. In today's world, more than ever, our success depends on us. We have to *make* our own opportunities. We have to make what we want to happen *happen*. Whether that is as a business owner or manager or worker, as a student, as an artist with a dream, as a volunteer devoted to a cause or a neighbor with a vision of what our community should be, as people who want something different and better for ourselves and our families—whatever that "different and better" means to us.

A second reason selling is the common thread to success is that selling is about much more than getting people to say "yes"— although the word "yes" is our goal and the most enjoyable part of selling. We will go beyond "yes" and talk about the opportunities we have to sell ourselves that might not seem like opportunities. A big chunk of selling is how we carry ourselves, our attitudes and our words and our actions, our energy, how we talk to people, and even more how we listen to them, so people like us and know what we do and remember us when some time in the future, they or somebody they know needs someone like us!

Everyone's in Sales: The Beginning

This is my second book. My first book is called *Everyone's in Sales* (published 2011), and what the title means is that every conversation—every interaction we have with everyone we meet every day—is a genuine, seize-it-right-now selling opportunity. That's because in every conversation, people are making decisions about us, and we want those decisions to be good ones.

We want people to decide "She's smart and passionate." Or "He knows how to listen and hear what I really need." Or "She knows how to get tough things done." Or "He's committed to excellence." Or "I can trust her to do right by me."

> *Every conversation and every interaction*
> *we have are selling opportunities.*

Another big theme of *Everyone's in Sales* is the idea of "Sales Culture." In organizations that have good Sales Cultures, everyone understands how what they do helps customers say "yes" and everyone knows the role they play in growing revenue and profits. Sales Cultures don't ask people to become sales professionals. Sales Cultures ask people to continue to do what they do well, to realize what they do truly impacts the bottom line, and to commit themselves to making customers and clients completely satisfied every time.

Everyone's in Sales talks about selling on the individual, team, and company levels, and how each level is important to building a good Sales Culture. Here's what these levels look like:

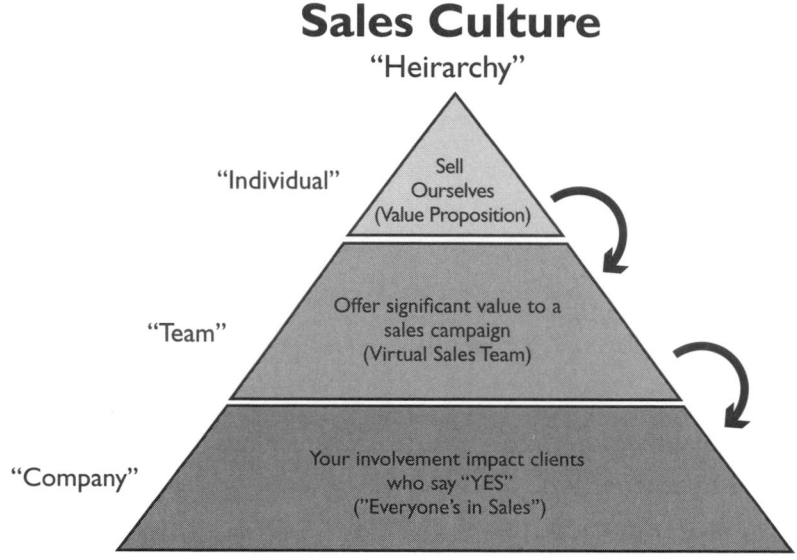

That was *Everyone's in Sales.* In this book, we're going to focus exclusively on us—sitting there on the top of the pyramid. Just like everything we do at work affects the success of our organizations, everything we do in our lives affects our success and happiness. Everything we do makes people want to say "yes" to us or not say "yes" to us. These people are bosses and colleagues and customers and our network as well as our friends and our neighbors and even our families. Please remember this! Everything we discuss in this book is founded on that simple fact.

Why Do We Need to Sell Ourselves? Because the World Has Changed Forever

All this is important because the world changed in 2008 and it's not changing back. It changed for me. I bet there's a pretty good chance it changed for you, too.

Before 2008, there were many more opportunities waiting for us in the world. And these opportunities were easier to enjoy. They were like a bowl of delicious ripe fruit sitting in front of us, and the only question we had to ask ourselves was "What do we want?"

We didn't need to be superstars. We didn't even need to be great at our work. Being good was good enough to get what we wanted. If we were comfortable with our jobs, we could feel confident those jobs would continue to be there for us because the economy was good.

To succeed now, we have to be good at
selling we are good at what we do.

Remember those times? Yes, I know, they were great. Poof! They're gone now. It's been a while since being good was good enough. Just being "technically proficient" at our work isn't a guarantee anymore. Being great isn't even a guarantee. Opportunities aren't calling us on the phone and asking, "Do you have a minute to talk?" We have to go find those opportunities and then sell ourselves to win them. This is even more true for people in professions where the work has shifted from full-time, permanent employment to outsourced consulting and temporary contracts and part-time projects adding up to a full-time job.

Yes, we are now "The Business of Us"—or pick another snappy phrase bouncing around that describes the new economy. To succeed in this economy, we have to sell ourselves well. And we can!

Here's How We Get Started

When I say things like "everyone's in sales" and "selling is the common thread to success" I usually get one of two reactions.

The first is a blank stare of pure terror. The second is a solid "I agree" nod followed by a look of confusion. I understand both reactions. I really do. And I understand that what I'm saying right now might sound scary, particularly if you think of yourself as a "non-professional sales person" or if you think selling is something you have to be born to do.

Selling can look scary. I promise you—it's not!

Selling can seem scary but I promise you—it's not! Once you start selling, you'll discover that you are good at it and that it's fun. So we're going to start by making you feel comfortable selling yourself and stop apologizing for doing it. Then we're going to build the personal qualities, especially the *confidence*, everyone needs to sell. We'll discuss the relationship skills all great sales people have. (Don't worry, I bet you've already got them and don't even know it!) We'll review simple selling principles that anyone can learn and that make selling easy and enjoyable. When we're done, you'll know how to make these principles work for you, too.

Finally, we'll talk about whether we are living in the "no" of the past or the "yes" of the future. That's because many of the opportunities we enjoyed yesterday don't exist today—and we have to recognize when these opportunities are gone, and find new ones to replace them, if we are going to get what we need, want, and deserve.

Sound good? Let's get started by answering these three questions:

Take Your Next Steps Now!

1. What are three things you *need*?

2. What are three things you *want*?

3. What are three things you *deserve*?

2

Stop Apologizing for Selling. It's How We Get What We Need, Want and Deserve!

The only time we should apologize for selling is when we sell ourselves short.

—Todd Cohen

The science on apologizing is fascinating. For me, the most fascinating work comes from Tyler Okimoto and his colleagues[1] who found that *not* apologizing made people feel better. People in their study who refused to apologize felt "empowered" and enjoyed greater feelings of "self-worth" and "integrity."

All this is great, and I would give it two thumbs up if it weren't for one problem: The people in this study actually had done something wrong. They just didn't want to admit it. That's not what I'm recommending. When we've done something wrong, we should admit it, make a sincere apology, and take responsibility. It's the right thing to do and it helps us become more successful. There's science on that, too.[2]

The thing about selling is that it is **not wrong**. We've just been taught it is wrong, which is what makes our Sales Apologists grow strong. Then they use that strength to stop us from getting what we want.

People become Sales Apologists because they think there is something "bad" about selling. They become Sales Apologists because they think selling is "easy" since good sales people make it look easy. They become Sales Apologists—and this reason bothers me the most—because they think there is something "wrong" with getting what they want. They think they don't *deserve* it.

We're throwing all these reasons out the window right now, along with our Sales Apologists. The only time we need to apologize is when we've made a mistake or done something wrong and we need to make amends. That's it.

From this sentence forward, we're going to start enjoying more of the integrity and self-worth Okimoto talks about, only we are going to enjoy them for the *right* reasons.

Why do people think selling is bad? Because popular culture gives sales people a bad rap. Watch an old Western on television and the guy in a fancy suit holding up a bottle of miracle medicine? What do they call this guy? A "snake-oil salesman." Say the words "used-car salesman" and what picture do you see in your head? Arthur Miller didn't win a Pulitzer Prize for writing **Life** *of a Salesman*. Leonardo DiCaprio didn't sell a bunch of tickets to a movie called *The* **Lamb** *of Wall Street*.

Why do people think selling is easy? Selling can look easy when it is done well. The sales professional sits down with a potential client. They have a conversation. At the end of the conversation, the client says "yes." Now behind that sales conversation is research and preparation and strategy and relationships and skill and experience we don't see. Because we don't see these things, we think selling is "easy" or comes "naturally" and so we don't value it as a profession.

The truth is that selling is work. It is work that everyone can do well, and not apologize for doing. And you can, too. I promise. One reason I can make this promise is because we are going to talk about selling *the right way*. We are going to understand the real needs of the people who can give us the "yes" we want. We're going to give good value for that "yes." We're going to listen. We're going to answer questions. We're going to be persistent to show we care. We will earn trust by showing we are committed to making people happy and satisfied every time. We're going to do this because:

> *When you sell the right way you*
> *never need to apologize.*

There is one more reason people become Sales Apologists: it's because they think they don't deserve to get what they want. I'm not going to make a long argument here. Let me just say one thing with complete conviction: We deserve to get what we want. We do.

I know men and women who are great at their work. But they don't get ahead as fast as they should—or get as far as they should—because they think they are not good enough.

The themes of this book are that selling is the common thread to success and that we should stop apologizing for being in sales. I believe that passionately. But there is one time when we should apologize for selling: *when we sell ourselves short.*

Ashamed of Selling: The Non-Profit Executive's Story

I think a lot about the executive at a large non-profit organization dedicated to fighting a disease. She said to me after one of my keynote addresses:

"I am tired of feeling I need to apologize for anything I do that seems like sales."

I think about her because her organization's success is rooted in her ability, and the ability of everybody around her, to sell—but shhh, don't tell. I think about her because her selling skills allow her non-profit to have a bigger impact: to fund more research, to provide more education and support programs, to get more people involved. I think about her because her ability to motivate and inspire and influence donors helps her organization help more people. Yet she sounded like she felt ashamed of her work.

You know what I think the problem was? I think she felt embarrassed about selling because—on some level—she believed that only things that have no value need to be sold.

Think about the examples from a few pages back. Snake oil. Used cars. Worthless stocks. That's what people think when they hear the word "sales."

On the other hand, people believe that good products, good services, good businesses, good ideas, good people sell themselves by the virtue that they're good and don't need any help doing it. That's simply not true. Especially nowadays. Mixed with that belief can be a feeling of entitlement, even hubris, which is worse, because few things will make people say "no" to us faster than the sense we think they owe us a "yes."

Good people, just like good companies, need to be sold well to succeed. "Sold well" doesn't mean special tricks or claims that aren't true or super-secret mind games. Sold well means we've understood people's real needs, and met those needs, and delivered something they value, and continue to deliver value every time.

> *Even great companies and great
> people don't sell themselves.*

Let's get back to our non-profit executive. Her organization offers donors and volunteers and supporters real value. Her non-profit is good at what it does. It make a measurable difference in the lives of the people it serves. Every dollar this non-profit spends makes an impact, and it spends those dollars wisely.

But donors and supporters don't just magically find this woman's organization because it is doing great work. Her selling begins with networking. She goes out every day and has conversations with as many people as she can—because remember, every conversation is a selling opportunity. From all the people she meets, she identifies those who might care about her organization's mission; maybe because that mission aligns with a business' goal or because they share a community. Maybe the donor has a personal passion for the non-profit's work.

Then she listens to the donors. She learns their needs and desires. She explains how her organization meets them. She builds and maintains relationships over years and years. She helps everyone win. Should she apologize for that? Definitely not!

We Don't Have to Be "Selfless" to Feel Good About Selling

You might think from my story about the executive's non-profit that I believe if we're selling to help other people, we are good. But if we are selling to help ourselves, and above all to make money, there is a problem. I don't think that and there's not!

I've worked at big for-profit companies during much of my career, and I speak at for-profit companies and non-profit organizations now. I got paid then. I get paid today. There's nothing wrong with making money. When we make money, that's a sign that we've helped someone. It's a sign that we've given them something they truly need or want. We've given them value. We've earned that money. And if we've really done our work well, people will thank us for selling them. Here's an example from my own life. I call it:

The Epic Saga of Todd and the Flat Screen TV

I have a floor on my house where I go to relax. Half the floor is devoted to my kitchen. I like cooking for family and friends. The other half of the floor is devoted to my television. I don't watch that many shows, but when I watch them, I like to enjoy them.

So I splurged and bought a fancy flat screen television and a big leather chair. I had the technology guys come and hang the television on the wall like a work of art, and the cable company came and got me connected.

I'm all set. I've got my television. I've got my chair. I sit back and turn on the TV. And I can't see the picture.

I break out the manual and spend hours adjusting the menus. I get nowhere. I move the chair around, but it doesn't help. The technology guys come back and they adjust the settings and run their diagnostics and they scratch their heads. I ask the cable company to come back. They check the wires and signals and they come up with nada.

Then I give up. I have a fancy television, but I can't see the screen.

Around that time, I decide my kitchen is too dark. I can't see when I'm cooking. So I ask for some recommendations and I have a company come out. I like the guy they send. His name is Mike and he's personable. Mike looks at my kitchen. He explains what's wrong and why. He explains how he would fix the problem. He gives me two choices at prices I think are fair. (Want people to say "yes" now? Give them two choices!) I say yes to one. He starts the work the same morning.

If we do our jobs really well, people
will thank us for selling them!

By lunch time, Mike's done. I turn on the lights in my kitchen and it's beautiful. I pay Mike happily. Mike thanks me. As he's getting ready to leave, Mike looks at my television and asks:

"Do you have trouble seeing the picture on that TV?"

Now the television isn't on. It is just hanging on the wall in the other room. But I tell him, "Yes. Oh you wouldn't believe. I tried everything!" Mike says to me:

"It's the lights in that room. No one ever installs them right."

Mike explains what's wrong and why. He explains how he would fix the problem. He gives me two choices at prices I think are fair. I say yes to one. He gets the work started that day and is done before dinner.

I turn on the television and I can see it. I sit down in my big chair and my shows look great. I am even happier than I was before. I pay Mike happily again.

Here's the moral of the story: When Mike looked at my television and asked that question, was he trying to sell me? Yes. Did

Mike get paid more for asking about my television? I sure hope so, because people like Mike make businesses successful. Was Mike acting like a salesman the day he came to my house? Yes. When Mike was acting like a salesman, was he doing anything differently than we would do normally? No. He was doing exactly what he always did. He was just thinking about it differently.

Is there anything Mike did that day in my house that wasn't honest and straight-forward and about helping me? No, not a thing. In fact, I was grateful to pay Mike more because he fixed a problem I didn't know how to solve.

Mike actually apologized for making me spend more money. I told him he'd helped me and made me happier. I told him not to apologize.

Mike is a great example of a person who sells the right way— the way we are going to discuss selling throughout this book. More importantly, Mike shows us how easy it is to become a Sales Apologist. Mike does a great job. He deserves to sell and to succeed. And not apologize for doing it!

Take Your Next Steps Now!

1. Think of the things you need, want, and deserve. Do you feel you need to apologize for wanting any of these things? If so, why?

2. Can you think of moments in your life when you felt you needed to apologize for selling yourself? What in those moments made you feel like apologizing? How would you act in those moments now?

3. Is there something you want that you aren't getting because it would involve selling yourself? Write down three ways you can sell yourself to get that thing.

NOTES

1. Okimoto TB, Wenzel M, Hedrick K. Refusing to apologize can have psychological benefits (and we issue no mea culpa for this research finding). *European Journal of Social Psychology.* 2013; 43:22-31.

2. A study conducted by researchers at the Ohio State University Fischer College of Business found that people wronged in a transaction are more likely to continue a business relationship if they get a sincere apology and the person in the wrong takes responsibility. That makes complete sense. That's what we want for ourselves and that's what we do when we've done something wrong. The study is Tomlinson EC, Dineen BR, Lewicki RJ. The road to reconciliation: Antecedents of victim willingness to reconcile following a broken promise. *Journal of Management.* 2004; 30(2):165-187.

3

Bring Our Passion to What We Sell

*Passion is energy. Feel the power that comes
from focusing on what excites you.*
— Oprah Winfrey

Let's talk about passion. I don't mean the kind we feel for another person. (Stay on topic, people!) I mean the passion we feel for what we do. Because one of the most effective selling tools I know is passion. More importantly, one of the surest signs I've seen of a person who is successful—or who is *going* to be successful—is passion.

Passion sells. When we believe in our hearts and guts that what we have to offer is of real value—what we make or what we do or the knowledge, skills, and experience we bring to our work—and we convincingly express that belief, then people will say "yes" to us. If we don't, they'll often say "no" even if we are excellent at what we do.

That is why we are starting here. We'll talk about how we *think* about making every interaction an effective selling opportunity.

But first we're going to look at how we need to *feel*. How we should feel begins with passion!

Science Says Passion Sells

It is said that just 7% of what people remember from a conversation is what we say. The words. How we say it—the sound of our voice and our body language—makes up the other 93%. Our passion and how we express it.

For the record, these percentages are based on communications research conducted by Professor Albert Mehrabian, and his studies do not come to those exact conclusions.[1] What Professor Mehrabian's work does state is that what we say and how we say it need to match in order for people to believe us. So the meaning of our words, and the emotions and attitudes we express while speaking those words, have to agree. If our words are saying one thing—and our attitude toward our words is saying something else—then people will believe our attitude.

For example, pretend you walk into the office of the vice president of a company and say, "I'm the best person for this project" but you say it in a mumbling voice while staring at your feet. What does this vice president think? Does she think you are the best person because those are the words you said? Or does she think you aren't the best because she barely heard you and you couldn't look her in the eye? According to Mehrabian, she'll listen to how you said the words—not the words you said—and then probably pick someone else for the job.

This insight of Professor Mehrabian's is important because it matches my experience as a real-life, knocking-on-doors, and closing-deals sales professional. I know when I became passionate about what I was selling I became more successful. I remember one client from a large pharmaceutical company in New Jersey who said to me, "I did not know anyone could get so excited about something so boring." The next thing he did was sign the order because he was riding the wave of my passion.

A Story about How Passion Sells

Recently, I was speaking in front of 800 high school students in a town in Western Pennsylvania. I invited one student to come on stage. This young man didn't know I was going to ask him to talk in front of hundreds of his classmates and he didn't know what he was going to say.

I asked if he liked his town. "Yes," he said. "What do you like about it?" I asked. The young man began describing all the great things about where he lived, how close the community was, how good the pizza was at a local restaurant. The more he talked, the more convinced I became I should live there, too—purely because he was passionate about his hometown and he expressed that passion.

This young man wasn't a professional sales person. He hadn't prepared what he was going to say. I could tell he was nervous, but the more he talked, the more relaxed he became. He showed that passion sells and that it is easy to sell when you are passionate about what you sell.

Is There a Difference Between Desire and Passion?

There is a difference between desire and passion in my mind, although I don't want to get too philosophical or start picking over the distinctions between one word and another. Let me tell you my meanings because I think they will make sense to you, though.

Desire is general and innate. It is wanting something better for ourselves. Passion is specific and can be developed. It's excitement about *how* we get that better, and enthusiasm about what that better *is*.

I started my career in sales. I had a desire to sell and to be successful. I studied the techniques. I learned everything I could from the people around me. I practiced and practiced my craft and I became good at it. I was passionate. My desire to be a good sales professional didn't help me become successful. Desire was simply my motivation. It was my passion to do my job well, which my clients felt, that helped me succeed.

The same thing is true in my current work. I'm passionate about helping people and companies build Sales Culture, and I'm passionate about helping you get what you deserve.

The other good news about desire and passion is that if you have desire, you can build passion. You can build passion by adopting the words, the actions, and the attitudes that express it. This is not "faking" passion. You can't fake passion because people will be able to tell you are faking. But you can make passion a choice and a commitment, and once you commit, you will feel it in your blood and bones. Your energy level will rise. You'll begin to feel excitement. The people around you will feel that excitement, too. And you'll be on your way.

How Passion Helps You Win

What is it about passion that is so persuasive? Passion sells.

Passion is partly about enthusiasm, and enthusiasm is contagious. If we are excited about who we are and what we do, then other people will become excited, too. They'll listen to us and they'll begin to think they should be as enthusiastic as we are.

Passion is also persuasive because a lack of passion hurts us when we are trying to sell. The words "I'm not passionate" are another way of saying, "I don't care." I think about my experiences flying on Southwest Airlines compared to other carriers, and I'll choose Southwest every trip I can because their people make me feel they really want my business and want to make sure I enjoy my flight. Their passion sells me, and it is also part of the good experience of flying with them.

How many times have you bought something from a person who didn't care about your business? Not many times, I'll bet. I'll also bet you swore you would never use that business again and went out of your way to find another one that could do the same thing. You might have even spent *more* money with another business rather than give it to one that didn't care about you. This is simple human nature, and human nature is real and powerful.

The same dynamic holds true in offices, in community groups, in volunteer organizations. Passion is contagious and makes people want to say "yes" to us. A lack of passion is equally catching and inspires people to say "no."

Another reason passion is so persuasive is that it is a highly reliable, though not 100% dependable, signal of excellence. People who love something tend to be good at it or know a lot about it.

For example, how many passionate baseball fans have you met who *can't* explain the infield fly rule or why 1-2 is a pitcher's count but 3-1 a batter's? Have you ever met someone who loves baking but whose cakes are inedible no matter how many glasses of milk you drink to help choke them down? Do you know a furniture maker who is passionate about his craft but in whose chairs you avoid sitting for fear they will burst apart and deposit you on the floor?

Play the odds and you'll find that most people who are passionate about their work or a cause or a subject are also experts in that subject. People who do what they love tend to do it well—and other people know this and feel it instinctively.

So passion is not just about making people *feel* good about who we are and what we do. It's about making them *think* good about us as well. Passion packs a wallop. Use yours to help you get what you want!

Take Your Next Steps Now!

1. Practice selling with passion right now. Pick something you care about—a hobby you enjoy, a sport you follow, a favorite restaurant—and talk with someone about all the reasons why you like it.

2. Now let's make it harder. Do the same thing without using the word "I." Not easy, is it? I want you to do this because when we sell, the focus should always be on the other person and not ourselves.

3. Finally, pick the part of your job you enjoy most and practice selling—with passion!—how your work delivers value to clients and helps your company succeed.

NOTES

1. Professor Mehrabian states his rule like this: Total Liking = 7% Verbal Liking + 38% Vocal Liking + 55% Facial Liking. So Professor Mehrabian's communications research is concerned with "feelings and attitudes" or liking and disliking, and how these are influenced by words, how the words are spoken, and the facial expression of the person speaking. It is this formula that has been over-generalized and over-interpreted, which doesn't mean it isn't useful or valuable. The two main studies of Professor Mehrabian are these:

    Mehrabian A, Wiener M. Decoding of inconsistent communications. *Journal of Personality and Social Psychology*. 1967; 6(1):109-114

    Mehrabian A, Ferris SR. Inference of attitudes from nonverbal communication in two channels. *Journal of Consulting Psychology*. 1967; 31(3):248-252

    As of the spring of 2014, you can find Professor Mehrabian's explanation of his research on his website: http://kaaj.com/psych/

4

Integrity: Doing the Right Thing Makes Us More Successful

With integrity you have nothing to fear,
since you have nothing to hide.
– Zig Ziglar

What is selling? The classic definition of selling is the work of matching buyers to sellers. I believe selling is bigger than that, but let's use this definition for now because it's relevant to selling and integrity. Selling matches buyers with sellers. It matches people who have a "yes" with people who want that "yes." It's as simple—and as complicated—as that.

Selling is both easy and complicated. The things we need to do to sell ourselves are easy. We know how to do them. You're probably doing them already. Using those skills in sales conversations is work, however. Buyers and sellers don't magically find each other. Buyers and sellers need sales people to bring them together; and the work of bringing them together takes time and knowledge and skill and discipline and determination. Selling is hard. We better bring our best game if we want to be successful. We better eat healthy and exercise and do our homework and wake up pumped every day if we want to get what we want.

Because selling is easy and hard, and because bringing buyers and sellers together is a real service that delivers real value, sales professionals get paid well.

There is a little problem with the words "paid well," though. Those words are the juicy apple that made the serpent of temptation slither into the paradise of capitalism. Those are the words that make some people forget sometimes they get paid well *to help buyers find the right sellers*. Those are the words that make a few people do anything—literally—because they think "getting paid" is their only goal.

This chapter isn't about that. It's about integrity. This book is about integrity. And I'm sure you're about integrity because if you weren't, would you have picked up a book telling you to stop apologizing for selling?

Let me tell you something else that is important if you are thinking, "I want to have integrity, but that apple is juicy and maybe having a little less integrity and a little more apple is okay sometimes."

Selling with integrity isn't about giving up money so we can feel good about ourselves or sleep better at night or have our grandmothers pat us on the head because we are such nice girls and boys who treat people nicely. Selling with integrity is about making *more* money, getting *more* of what we want, enjoying *more* success. We might not become successful quite as fast. We might not watch our income go BOOM! But we'll never see it go BUST either. We won't ever find ourselves in orange jumpsuits, shackled up, and staring blankly at the smoking ruins of our lives because we earned our success the wrong way.

Good sales people are patient. They know selling is about when their customers want to say "yes" and not when they want their customers to say "yes." Good sales people value long relationships over a quick boost to revenue. Good sales people are truly interested in what their clients do and what their clients want, which I think is the essence of networking. Most of all, good sales people make good money and get ahead by helping people. Do you know what else? When we get ahead helping people, those people will help us get ahead in return.

The Bedrock of Integrity Is *Respect*

Respect is the foundation on which integrity is built. Respect for ourselves. Respect for our clients and other people. Respect for the interactions we have with them. When we respect ourselves and others, we believe everyone has value and deserves to be treated fairly. When we respect an interaction—say, a sales interaction—we're saying that interaction has value and we should act fairly within it.

The first person we should respect in a sales conversation is ourselves. Respect yourself and respect what you do! Recognize the time it took you to develop your skills and knowledge, to do the work on a project, to understand the needs of a client or colleague or boss. Give yourself the credit you earned and deserve, and use that credit to build your energy and passion. Especially use your self-respect to motivate you to ask for a thing you want—a sale, a job, a raise, a contribution—because you've earned the opportunity to ask. You deserve the opportunity to ask.

We need to respect our customers. This advice is obvious, but the benefits are not. When we respect people, they will tell us what we need to do to make them say "yes." When we respect people, we build relationships that will help us succeed for years to come. Clients and colleagues and bosses become rock-solid friends; friends become rock-solid professional partners.

Respect is important because respect is a *feeling* and feelings are the most powerful communication tools we have, as any storyteller (or marketing professional) will tell you. Feelings create instant connections with people. Feelings are memorable. Long after we have forgotten why we liked a childhood teacher, we remember we liked her. Feelings persuade. Emotions sell because emotions drive our decisions more than reasons do. People feel we respect them and respect ourselves, and they trust those feelings.

And please remember this insight: Respect is about the words "we" and "us" not the words "me" or "them." When we build a relationship on respect, there are no sides. There is simply a collaboration in which each person has the natural expectation of being treated fairly and the natural responsibility to treat the other person fairly. Respect is a feeling, an attitude, and a commitment. When we express respect through our actions, people look at us and say, "He has integrity" and "She has integrity."

When we do this, selling is easy. When we do this, selling is fun. When we do this, we don't feel the least urge to apologize because we know we are selling the *right* way. When I feel that I've really earned the trust of a client, I get excited—I even feel butterflies sometimes—because it is such a great compliment.

We Know to Sell with Integrity. Let's Go Do It!

I'm not trying to be flip, but unless we are psychopaths—which means we plain-old don't understand the rules of social behavior— we already know how to sell with integrity because we know how to do everything with integrity.

When we do what we promise, we have integrity. When we are honest with a person, even when telling the truth is not to our advantage, we have integrity. When we can be trusted to do the right thing when no one is looking, we have integrity.

Integrity goes hand in hand with a strong sense of personal responsibility. We believe it is *our* job to make things happen. We don't point our fingers or shrug our shoulders when they don't happen. When we make a mistake, we apologize (one of the times when we *should* apologize) and we make it right. When we fall short of expectations, we recognize that and fix it. We don't pass the buck. We hold onto it. We hold ourselves to tough standards because people with integrity have high expectations for themselves.

You can see now why integrity is a powerful and easy-to-use selling tool. Remember in Chapter 2, we talked about how when we sell the right way, we never have to apologize. We can also say that selling with integrity is selling the right way. It's the very best kind of selling. Because the heart of selling is about more than deals. It's about more than process and technique and strategy and checklists and algorithms applied to a database. It's about more than psychology. It's about more than looking good and feeling good. All these things are important. We should do them to get what we need, want, and deserve. Guilt-free.

The best sale is not the sale we make happen, though. The best sale is the sale that *happens to us* when we immerse ourselves in helping customers and colleagues and bosses and business partners and collaborators and friends and neighbors. When we do that—and how we do that is by acting with *integrity*—then what we want will come to us.

People will say "yes" to us and be happy to do it. People will thank us for giving them the opportunity to say "yes." People will feel good about saying "yes" because they can help us while helping themselves. There is nothing like getting a good deal you can feel good about taking. How do you make that happen? Act with integrity. That's not complicated. That's simple!

Take Your Next Steps Now!

1. Was there a moment in your career when telling the truth felt like a risk and you told it anyway? How did it work out?

2. Think about a time someone treated you with integrity. How long ago was it? Would you still work with this person today?

5

Confidence:
The Supreme Tool of All Selling!

With confidence, you can pull off pretty much anything.
— Katy Perry

Even more than passion and integrity, confidence is the difference-maker in sales.

How important is confidence? Even research has shown that people pay more attention to confidence than they do to results (which surprised me and I'm a believer in confidence). Don Moore of Carnegie Mellon University in Pittsburgh found that people are more willing to follow the recommendations of a confident person than a person who lacks confidence, even when the confident person is frequently wrong.[1]

Cameron Anderson, a psychologist from the school of business at Berkeley, devised an experiment that demonstrated people value confidence at least as much as they value competence, and that the most influential individuals in a group tended to be those with the most confidence as opposed to the people with the most knowledge or ability.[2]

I'm not recommending we replace our expertise with confidence, of course. We have to be truly good at what we do to be successful. But if anything reinforces the idea that selling ourselves is essential to success, it is the work of Moore and Anderson.

Confidence is related to passion. Passion is *loving* what we do. Confidence is *knowing* we are great at what we do. Confidence comes from having reasons and information and facts at our command that prove it.

People feel our confidence like they feel our passion and see integrity in our actions. And like passion and integrity, confidence persuades. Confidence sells and makes selling easy. Confidence is even more powerful than passion, though, because while people feel our passion, they can both feel our confidence and put it to the test. Confidence is even more powerful than integrity because while integrity assures people we will do the right thing, confidence tells them we will deliver the right results.

How do people put our confidence to the test? By asking us questions. Hard questions. Smart questions. Challenging questions. By asking us "show me the money" questions. By saying, you've got my attention. You've got my interest. Now sell me. Show me. Convince me. Prove it to me. Close me. Getting what we need, want, and deserve comes down to that. And it is the most fun we'll ever have because getting what we want is fun.

Maybe that sounds a little scary. All of us can do it, I promise, because confidence isn't a magic elixir the gods gave some of us to drink as babies and everyone else is out of luck. Winning isn't something that happens to some people and not others and no one knows why. We can build our confidence when we need it, as long as we are ready to do one thing.

How Do We Build Confidence? Do Our Homework!

That's the great news about confidence. We can get it by doing our homework. And we all know we all can do homework because we've all done it for school. Building confidence is absolutely in our control.

Saying we all can do that homework is not the same thing as saying that homework is easy. Or that it's only going to take a few hours. Or that all the answers will drop out of the sky like apples from a tree that just needs a little shaking.

Homework is *work* and we have to do a lot of it to build the bedrock of our confidence. The place we begin is with ourselves. Where there is knowledge or experience or skills we need to reach our goals, we have to go get them first.

Then we have to explain why we're the best at what we do. As a result, we need to know our *value propositions*, which is a topic so important it has its own chapter in this book. Our value propositions are our most powerful arguments for why people should engage with us, work with us, and say "yes" to us. Behind these value propositions, we'll want facts, results, numbers, concrete examples, stories with emotions, and measurable outcomes that show what we say is true. Even more importantly, our actions have to prove our value propositions are true.

For example, pretend you are a project manager and your value proposition is "I consistently get complex projects done right, on tight deadlines, and on budget." Sounds good, right? Behind that, you'll want to have examples of projects you've done that demonstrate those qualities. Imagine you have five projects that show you are as good as you say you are. These projects make you comfortable selling. You feel relaxed. You feel energized. You feel ready. You feel—that's right—confident.

Our homework begins with us and it continues with the person who has the "yes" we want. Remember I said that selling is matching the needs of "buyers" with what "sellers" provide. Our first homework assignment is to find out whether our "buyer" has a need for what we are selling. That might be our skills and experience as a candidate for a new job. That might be a role in a community play or a donation from a business to support our local school. There are many buyers in our lives.

Knowing whether our person with the "yes" is interested can be hard, and selling is not a simple straight-line process, even though we are discussing it step by step in this book. For our purposes here, let's say when a person with the "yes" is not interested, we move on to the next opportunity—and there is always a next opportunity. If the answer is "yes," then we go into research mode. We find out everything we can about the person or people who will make the decision. We learn all we can about what they really need and want. We learn about our competitors. And so on.

Everything that helps us understand the needs of our "buyer" will help us because we have information we can use to sell and because having this information gives us confidence!

Doing All This Homework Prepares Us to (a) Talk or (b) Listen?

This isn't a trick question. We've done our homework and built our confidence so when we sit down with a potential customer, we are prepared to . . . listen.

Old sales hands say one of the most important sales skills is listening well, and that if we are talking more than other people, we've got a problem. If we are listening more and having a real conversation, on the other hand, we are off to a great start.

When we are relaxed, when we are comfortable, when we are confident, it is easy to listen well. That's because we aren't worried about what the person is going to say or what we are going to say. We have a solid grasp of the general "facts" of the conversation. As a result, we can focus on the specifics of what our buyer is saying, and ask smart questions, and work to understand in detail what she really needs and wants.

This is powerful because people want to say "yes" to people who understand them and are committed to helping them rather than just helping themselves. When we listen well, we do that, and we make it enjoyable to work with us, and we build trust, and most of all, we gain the information we need to make a sale. Because our "buyer" has told us what she *really* needs. Then all we have to do is put together reasons for why we are the people to choose.

A "Confidence Is Selling" Story

I have a friend—we'll call him Larry—who had a client that needed 50 complicated maintenance projects done at a manufacturing facility. The client really wanted Larry to complete all 50 projects at once, and was putting pressure on Larry to do it that way.

Larry knew from his experience that working on five projects at a time would give the client the best results. Larry took the sales conversation step by step. He listened. He explained why his approach worked. Then Larry used his confidence to close the deal: "I've been doing this a long time, sir, and I know this is the best way to get the results you want."

The outcome? Larry completed the 50 jobs and then identified five more projects after that, and then five more; and Larry eventually completed 600 projects with this client. Larry's confidence was not the whole story, of course. His company did excellent work.

And each time, Larry did right all the things good sales people do. Larry's confidence, though, was the difference-maker.

Confidence Helps Us Sell Every Step on the Way to "Yes"

Confidence helps us do more than listen well. The first thing confidence does is help us not apologize for selling! When we feel good about what we do—when we know we genuinely help people—we don't apologize because we having nothing to apologize for.

Doing our homework and building our confidence makes it easy to handle a question we can't answer. This is because confidence makes us comfortable being vulnerable. For example, it makes it easy to say:

> *"I don't have an answer to that question right now. Give me a day and I'll get back to you with one."*

That's a great answer and it builds trust (unless we answer every question asked like that!). People want to be told the truth, and people are a little suspicious of someone who always has all the answers. If we can answer eight out of every ten questions we are asked, nine out of every ten, we're rock stars of selling. We shouldn't go for ten out of ten unless we really do have the answer. Otherwise, we'll make people wonder about our answers to the other nine questions.

Confidence prepares us to sell with conviction, to *know* and *feel* what we are saying is true and make our buyer feel that conviction. Remember Professor Mehrabian's research that we discussed in the passion chapter, on how the meaning of our words and the emotions we express speaking those words need to match. They need to be "congruent"—if you'll let me use a 50-cent word here. When our words and feelings don't match, when we say, "I'm the best person for this project!" but we don't sound confident, then what our buyers hear is that we are not the best person. People will hear a lack of confidence—intensely and intuitively—and make decisions against us.

Confidence prepares us to hear, understand, and react to objections. Objections are a natural part of sales conversations, so much so we'll spend a chapter discussing how to handle them. For now, know we will hear objections and confidence will help us handle them well.

Confidence helps us hold our ground when we are negotiating. Another natural part of business is that everyone is trying to get a good deal. Our buyers want to get the best agreements they can. We want to get the best agreements we can. That's fair, and it is one of the things that makes selling fun. At its best, selling is a conversation in which each side has rights and responsibilities—to be treated fairly and to treat the other person fairly in return. When we know that, and we know we are a good match for a buyer, it makes it easier for us to say "no" to requests in a way that's effective and graceful. Sometimes, the right "no" is more powerful than any "yes" because it shows we have confidence in our work. We know we are the best people. That gives us confidence, and confidence sells!

Finally, confidence helps us keep our energy high and our focus tight and our attitude upbeat, optimistic, and constructive when we are in a tough sales conversation. We're all human beings, and sometimes we are going to feel frustration with an interaction and want to let it show. Maybe we feel that we are not being taken seriously and that makes us mad and we want to show we're mad. Maybe we feel we are not being treated right and our ego wants to jump into the boxing ring and start throwing punches. The people my dad called "a class act" don't do that. It's hard sometimes, I know. When we have confidence, though, it's much easier to stay cool, stay positive, and keep working toward "yes."

Take Your Next Steps Now!

I. Do you have three stories that you can tell that show you're great at what you do? If you do—go tell them to someone you trust.

2. Did you sell with these stories? If not, what was the problem? Was it the stories themselves? Your delivery? Both?

3. If you don't have stories—or you didn't feel good about the ones you told—now is the time to get to work. If you feel stuck, read the "Value Propositions" chapter and come back here.

4. Tell your stories again. How did you do this time?

NOTES

1. Don Moore's research is reported in the article "Humans prefer cockiness to expertise" by Peter Aldhous in June 10, 2009 issue of *The New Scientist*.
2. Cameron Anderson's research is reported in the article "The confidence gap" by Katty Kay and Claire Shipman in the May 2014 issue of *The Atlantic*. The entire article is well worth reading!

6

Have a Goal. Make a Plan. Commit. Act.

There must be foresight, system, planning and honest purpose, as well as perspiration.
—Thomas A. Edison

I know "have a goal" is familiar advice. I know "make a plan" is as dry as chapter topics come. "Act" is a good word if I'm selling sneakers. I'm selling that selling is the common thread to success. And my goal is to do this by talking about things you haven't heard a hundred times.

All that said, I would be guilty of major selling malpractice if we didn't talk about having clear goals, making a plan, and following through. Because from my years in sales and building Sales Cultures, I know that we need good plans to be successful at selling.

In business, these plans need to be well researched, precisely defined, carefully considered, and consistently executed. For ourselves, we don't have to make them 100 pages or even 10 pages long. We just need the plan to be smart, make sense, have concrete steps to follow, and have measurable objectives so we can tell when we are making progress. Most of all, our plans need a goal!

I promise this will be quick, painless, valuable, and fun—especially if you are brand-new to selling. When we're done, you'll be one step closer to selling like a pro.

Step 1. What Is It You Want—*Exactly?*

The key to that question is the word "exactly" and what I mean by the word "exactly" is this: Can we tell people what we want—clearly, briefly, specifically, and powerfully—so they understand what our goals are and can think of ways to help us get them?

Take a job search question, for instance, and compare these two examples. #1: "I need a better job that pays more money." #2: "I'm looking for a job as a regional sales manager in the medical technology, medical device, or pharmaceutical industries." Which one of these examples is better? Which one shows people we have thought hard about our career? Which one makes them think we have the skills, experience, focus, and determination to get it? Which one makes it easy to remember us and our goal and brainstorm ways to help us achieve it? Example #2 by a mile, hands down.

Our goals don't have to be focused on pure business. Maybe we have a daughter who is a great musician and she has her heart set on going to a major performing arts school and we want to help her. Saying "I want to help my daughter get into a good music school" is fine. Saying "I want to know what we need to do to give my daughter the best chance of being accepted at Julliard" is better.

This step is simple, and doing it right makes an enormous difference in how successful we are at selling. It shows we are smart and serious. And it makes it easy for people to join our "virtual sales teams," which is an idea I talk about during my Sales Culture keynotes. These teams are all those customers, clients, bosses, colleagues, friends, neighbors, and family members who want to help us achieve our goals—if they know *exactly* what those goals are!

Step 2. What Do We Need—and Especially *Who* Do We Need—to Succeed?

Think of this as the "market research" step. We've got a specific goal—our "product development" step. Good. Now what do we need to reach that goal? Let's go back to the regional sales manager job example. Do we have the skills, experience, and results that make us a strong candidate for the position? If we need something to make a strong selling case for ourselves, then we need to go get it. Remember, selling is about matching the needs of buyers and sellers. When what we are selling—ourselves—is a good match for the needs of our "buyers," then we have a better chance of succeeding.

The same is true of our Julliard example. We might find out that attending a summer music camp will improve our daughter's chances, so we get her into the camp. Let's consider another example. We want help from our local representative to clean up our park. We find that showing strong community interest and organization will get the attention of the local politicians, so we go out and do that. This is "homework" like we discussed in the last chapter.

Maybe even more important than what we need is *who* we need. This group includes our "buyers": those people who can give us the "yes" we want. It also includes people who know how to find new "buyers" for us.

This second group is important because they are the *every conversation, every interaction we have with everyone we meet every day is a genuine selling opportunity* group. You would be surprised by who knows who. I've been surprised plenty of times in my life. These moments are our best chances to take advantage of resonance and timing. By resonance, I mean connecting with people through messages and emotions. Timing is resonating with the right person at the right moment.

Our "buyers" are our target market, and the people who can help us find these buyers are our network. Our target market is obviously important because these are the people who can say "yes" to us. My Sales Culture viewpoint is that our network is equally important. We don't always realize someone we know is actually a buyer. We definitely don't know that many buyers are one connection away from our network, our virtual sales team, everyone we know who can help us.

Step 3. What Are We Going to Do? When Are We Going to Do It?

This is the "sales plan" part of your personal sales campaign. We know who we want to sell. How are we going to sell them?

First, we focus on relationships. There are kinds of selling where we close buyers fast: A lot of retail selling is like that, for example. Customers walk into a store and they buy or they leave and don't come back. (Big purchases—new cars, for example—are different.)

Selling ourselves is much more about building relationships than making cash registers ring, and building relationships takes time. You probably have heard the famous phrase that people need to "know, like, and trust us" before we get their business. That's extraordinarily true when what we sell is ourselves.

Building these relationships requires a little finesse and delicacy, and everybody can do it. The trick is to plan different interactions or "touches" (in-person, phone, email, social media, even paper mail) over a period of time. Make sure those interactions are valuable to our "yes" people. Study their reactions and adjust accordingly. Every person is different. Some people like to interact via email. Great. Some people never want to see an email. Great, too. For some people, calling them every day for a month will make them want to hit us with a rolled up newspaper. Others will admire our determination and eventually talk to us. As a friend of mine says:

"One person's diligence is another person's stalking. Knowing which is the trick!"

Create a calendar with a schedule of touches, keep notes on the results, adjust what you do based on how people respond, always decide what will be your next step, and keep at it. Professional sales people will recognize this as what they do all day, every day with help from customer relationship management software (CRMs). You don't need to get that elaborate. Just be positive. Be pro-active. Be persistent. Commit. Act!

Step 4. Is It Working? Yes? Good. No? Try Something New

In my life, I've had many sales ideas that I believed passionately would work. Some worked great. Some worked okay. Some didn't work at all. That's why measuring progress is key—because it's hard to know what will sell until we try. And we want to know what isn't selling, so we can try something else!

What looks like "progress" that isn't a flat-out "yes"? When our selling is focused on relationships, then conversations, interactions, and responses are all measures of progress. Are people talking to us? Are we getting coffee meetings? Are people calling *us* with questions? Are they coming to us with opportunities or ideas?

All these are tangible measures of progress. At some point, we need to get a "transactional" value from the relationship: a referral, an offer, an opportunity, a "yes." Chances are that "yes" will take a lot longer than we want. Always stay optimistic. But always keep your eye on tangible measures of success, too. Be patient, just not endlessly patient. Have a goal. Make a plan. Commit to it. Act. React. Revise. Keep going. And success will come!

Take Your Next Steps Now!

1. Do you have clear, specific goals? Do they make sense to other people? Test your goals on someone you trust.

2. To make a plan, start with a calendar and a spreadsheet. Add names and activities to the calendar. Record what you do and the response on the spreadsheet.

3. After a month or two, add ratings next to your names. Focus more on the people you rate highly. Find new names to add to your plan!

7

What Do We *Really* Do? Our Value Propositions

Price is what you pay. Value is what you get.
—Warren Buffet

A powerful, persuasive, memorable, and resonant value proposition is one of the most essential selling tools we have.[1] What is it? Our value propositions express the most compelling reason why people should listen to us, engage with us, remember us, help us, work with us, and say "yes" to us. At their best, value propositions express *why* we do what we do. When we use our value propositions well, our actions demonstrate we are committed to the values they express.

A value proposition is short and sweet. It is clear and concise. (Seven words—or less—is best.) A value proposition is instantly understood by everybody everywhere. Our value propositions should be about us—not our current jobs or current companies or products and services. As a result, they should speak equally to people in our professional and our personal lives.

Our value propositions should resonate by engaging emotions and promising we can solve problems. Our value propositions should be intriguing. We want them to capture the imagination.

We want our value propositions to spark interest, to make people ask us questions and to start conversations. This is especially important if we are networking to find new clients or a new job for ourselves. Conversations are selling opportunities. A good value proposition helps us start more.

Creating value propositions that do all these things might sound like a pretty tall order. They are well worth the time to create, however! Let's look at some examples:

> **A receptionist**: I make people feel welcome and important.
> **A process expert:** I make little changes that create big savings.
> **An airline pilot**: I transport people safely, comfortably, and on time.
> **A marketing consult:** I make marketing dollars earn more money.
> **A doctor:** I make people feel cared for.
> **A cleaning person:** I make people proud of our company.
> **My father:** I make people smile.

As you might guess, I like my dad's value proposition the best. My father was a wedding photographer and he understood people wanted to remember their wedding days as "perfect." He did everything he could to make sure that happened. When people were smiling in the photos he took, he knew they would remember their wedding as perfect.

I Don't Have a Value Proposition. "I'm Just the . . ."

I believe this is the most important thing I say during my keynote addresses: *nobody* is "**just the** [fill in this blank with a job title]."

Everyone counts. Everyone matters. Everyone working at an organization contributes to the success of that organization, whether he or she knows it or not.

Everyone counts. Everyone matters. I say these words a lot. I say them because I believe them passionately and because I've seen what happens when people embrace them. People who are barely hanging on—or doing "okay maybe"—start to excel. They start to enjoy success. They start to earn the rewards they deserve.

Let me tell you a story about one of the value propositions we just saw.

A cleaning person: I make people proud of our company.

I was speaking at a printing company about Sales Culture. A woman named Karen raised her hand and said to me, "I don't do those things. I just drive the cleaning machine around the plant."

When the plant is clean every morning, how do people feel? I asked. "They feel good about where they work," she said. When customers come to tour your company, what do they think when they see your facilities are well maintained? "They think they should work with us!" she said.

Then Karen told me she also ran the loading dock, and I asked her how important it was that their customers got the right jobs delivered to them on time. "Very important," she replied.

Karen played critical roles in helping her company succeed. She just didn't see them. Karen didn't have what I call "a direct line of sight to revenue." She didn't see how what she did helped her company make money. Once she did, she realized she mattered. And everyone else realized she mattered, too.

So let me say this with total conviction: If you think you don't have a value proposition, you do. What you do matters. What you do counts.

Why: The Key to an Inspiring Value Proposition

The most inspiring value propositions focus on *why* we do what we do. The TEDx video to watch is Simon Sinek's "How Great Leaders Inspire Action." Sinek just briefly mentions value propositions in the video, and yet he gets to the heart of what our value propositions should be when he asks:

> *"What is your purpose, your cause, your belief? . . . Why do you get out of bed in the morning, and why should anyone care?"*

When we say our value propositions should "resonate" and "inspire," what we mean is that they should make an emotional connection with people by answering those questions.

When we do, then people choose us because we share their beliefs and values. "People don't buy what you do. They buy why you do it," Sinek says. "What you do is simply the proof of what you believe." Our actions prove our value propositions are true.

My father believed he should help everyone live a good life. For the people at the weddings he photographed, this meant helping them remember an important day as "perfect." For the people my father relied on to do his job well, it was making sure they were successful so he could be successful—which included helping the man who sold him film stay in business when this man's cash flow got tight. For my family and mother and me, that meant giving us his love and respect and attention and pride and support every day so we could be successful and happy. That's what my father believed. That's *why* he did what he did. What he did—as Sinek says—simply proved it. He made people smile.

Why You Need a Value Proposition

Now that we know what value propositions are, let's talk about *how* value propositions help us sell ourselves better.

Value propositions speed up communication. When we clearly express our value to companies, clients, friends, neighbors—so they understand the first time we tell them—every conversation becomes a more *effective* sales conversation.

What are the results? If our goal is to increase awareness of our value to an organization—and so increase our job security—that awareness increases more quickly. If we want new clients for our business, we convert more people into leads. If we are looking for a job, we sell ourselves better. If we want people to support our cause, we get more of them to listen and agree to help.

Another benefit of value propositions, when we know them word-for-word stone-cold, is that we can articulate them with confidence, at any time, in any situation.

Remember those words from earlier chapters? Confidence. Passion. Energy. We talked about these things because the greatest value propositions in the world mean nothing if we deliver them without conviction, if we stumble over the words we say.

Knowing exactly what our value propositions are—and believing in them passionately—makes selling ourselves with them easier.

Most importantly, having persuasive value propositions helps other people help us because they understand *how* to help. They understand what we do. They understand the value we offer. They understand who is most likely to need that value. They are inspired to help because they know how to talk about us. The result? More people who will talk about us when they meet someone who needs something we know how to do well.

Now let's sit down and write our value propositions.

Defining What We *Really* Do Can Be *Really* Hard

I did mention writing value propositions isn't easy, yes? If you are having a hard time writing yours, don't feel bad and don't give up.

Big companies have teams of experienced professionals who research and analyze and brainstorm and refine, and refine again, their value propositions over a long period of time before they find messages that are clear, powerful, backed by facts, and resonate with their target markets and customers. All we might have is a piece of paper, a pencil, and the desire to get going.

The best place to start—and I recommend this even if you have a good grasp of your value propositions—is to ask people you trust, "What do I *really* do for you?"

> "*Resonating value propositions are very effective, but they are not easy to craft.*" —Harvard Business Review

One of the ideas I talk about frequently is "vulnerability is nobility." What I mean is when we make ourselves vulnerable, when we ask someone we trust to help us see our strengths as well as our weaknesses, we get incredibly valuable information and insights.

Some of the most important conversations I've had in my life have begun when I've made myself vulnerable and asked, "What is it you think that I do?" I asked that question to an important sales consulting client of mine and he told me, "You've helped us build our Sales Culture."

That's right. The value proposition for my business? It was a gift from someone I trusted that he gave me after I made myself vulnerable.

You want to ask that question to people from your professional life. Maybe people you are working with now. Maybe people you have worked with in the past. I would especially recommend making yourself vulnerable and asking your boss or an important client or your mentor.

Asking the "What do I really do for you?" question can be scary. I'm an old-school believer in face-to face conversations but if that feels too hard, pick three people, ask them if you can send them an email with the question, and see what happens. This is the one I use sometimes and you can use it, too:

Dear [person's name] -

I would like to ask you to take a few minutes to answer one question for me. **That question is "What is it do you think I do?"**

Your response can be as brief or as verbose as you like. Please note this is for me to learn about myself and my role.

Thanks in advance for taking the time!

Regards,

Todd

The chances are pretty good you won't receive an "Aha! That's it exactly!" insight from the first person you ask. You're more likely to get many different comments. Take them all seriously. Write down your own thoughts without censoring yourself. Then sort similar comments into groups and themes. Think, write, revise, and test your ideas on people you trust. Then rethink, rewrite, re-revise, and retest your ideas again.

Focus on using actions words that have energy. If you can, quantify some of your value propositions with measureable results. For example, look at this value proposition again:

A process expert: I make little changes that create big savings.

If you are that process expert and can say, "I make little changes that reduce costs by 20%"—and you have the data to back up that claim—then say that. Specifics, hard numbers, and real results are things that add big muscle to a value proposition.

Keep in mind that value propositions feel hard to write because the best ones are simple, obvious, and powerful. Think of my dad's value proposition again: "I make people smile." He didn't come up with that during the first wedding he photographed. He found it after thinking deeply about the value of his work and listening to what people told him.

Some Value Proposition Insights from
the *Harvard Business Review*

James Anderson, James Narus, and Wouter van Rossum published an article titled "Customer Value Propositions in Business Markets" in the *Harvard Business Review* that looks at best practices for value propositions.[1]

I like this article because it states *"value propositions can be a guiding beacon as well as the cornerstone for superior business performance,"* which means our value propositions point us toward good opportunities as well as help sell.

The article breaks down value propositions into three categories. The first is "all benefits," which is every reason a person should say "yes" to us. The second is "favorable points of difference," which are all the reasons people should say "yes" to us rather than someone else. The third is "resonating focus," which concentrates on the one or two most important reasons people should say "yes" to us rather than someone else.

As you might guess, Anderson and his co-authors found that value propositions with a resonating focus work best because they got to the heart of the qualities that "**mattered most**" to people and were "**simple yet powerfully captivating**." Anderson and his co-authors also emphasize that value propositions should focus on ways we can help people "**solve problems**." These are the qualities I've found help me sell.

The authors say we need to "demonstrate and document" the claims our value propositions make. Proving we are good is as critical to selling as having value propositions that powerfully express why we are good.

Finally, I want to highlight the word "resonating." From re-inventing my career after the Great Recession, I know how important it is for value propositions to resonate with people. The first ones I used did not resonate and it was difficult to begin conversations using them. Once my value propositions resonated, my business began to take off.

A Few Things Your Value Proposition Should *Not* Be

I have found it helpful to point out a few things a value proposition should *not* be. Your personal value proposition should *not* be the title on your business card. If you have your card handy, take it out, cross out your title, and leave the card marking this page. Your value proposition should *not* be a list of skills, experience, technical competencies, or certifications. It should *not* have any vague language, technical jargon, complicated acronyms, or stale clichés, either.

There you have it. I don't think there is a better way to end this chapter than to encourage you to—

Take Your Next Steps Now!

1. Identify three people who you want to ask the key value proposition question: "What is it I really do?" Then go ask them.

2. Why do you do what you do? Why should people care?

3. Use the answers to the questions above and write three different value propositions. Share them with people you trust.

4. Practice speaking your value propositions. Keep practicing until they feel easy and comfortable.

NOTES

1. Many places in this chapter I reference "Customer value propositions in business markets" by James Anderson, James Narus, and Wouter van Rossum, published in the March 2006 issue of the *Harvard Business Review*.

8

The Selling Skills
We Already Have
(and Don't Know It)!

You don't close a sale, you open a relationship.
—Patricia Fripp

People think selling involves complicated strategies, sophisticated techniques, and deep psychological insights. For top sales professionals, it does. The best sales people are like chess grandmasters. Their game is so deep we don't realize they are selling until we find ourselves signing on the dotted line.

The good news is that we don't need to be sales professionals to sell ourselves well. The most effective selling skills are ones we already possess. All we need to do is recognize they are selling skills, and use them consistently. We don't have to do anything differently. We just have to think differently about what we do.

These selling skills fall into two categories. The first is relationship skills. The second is simply being good at what we do. Let's talk about relationship skills first.

Our Plan for Relationship Selling— aka "Focus on the Other Person"

"People like to do business with people" may be the selling principle we hear most often, unless it is "people do business with people they know, like, and trust." We've all heard these ideas many times. In fact, both reached the dreaded status of cliché decades ago.

We hear these ideas because they are profoundly true and because they are apparently easy to forget—based on the number of people who seem to think the key to success is building lousy relationships.

So let me give a shout-out to relationship building. Then let me say we build relationships *by helping other people*. When we do that, we'll sell and we'll succeed.

My relationship selling plan is all about attitudes and behaviors that make focusing on other people easier. Here they are.

Start with Ego Control and Humility

Confidence is essential to selling. Confidence is a powerful, productive quality in sales. But sometimes, in some people, confidence comes with robust self-esteem (to put it nicely) or with arrogance and abrasive over-confidence (to speak plainly).

An obvious problem with arrogance is that it turns people off. If people know us and don't like us, chances are good we will not get their business regardless how excellent our work is. A less obvious problem with arrogance is that arrogant people want the focus to be on them. To sell effectively, we have to focus on other people.

We all deserve to have our self-esteem validated, and there are times and places where it should be. These times and places just aren't selling conversations. So I check my ego at the door before I walk in a room. I put my ego in a drawer before I pick up the phone or write an email. This is taking the "high road of vulnerability." Just like making ourselves vulnerable by asking "What is it you think I really do?" pays dividends, being vulnerable in sales conversations also pays. I encourage you to do it.

A related concept is the idea of being humble in our relationships. Being humble does not mean we avoid demonstrating our skills, knowledge, ability, and experience when these things can help the other person. What being humble means is that we do not use these interactions as opportunities to show off. Even more to the point—if someone knows what we know or can do what we do, they won't bother talking to us because they don't need us. Since it is natural for us to have expertise the other person does not have in sales conversations, we should behave naturally and humbly as a result.

There's a great quote from the Phillies second baseman, Chase Utley, that applies:

> *"My dad always told me you don't need to tell people how good you are. If that's the case, people will tell you."*

There is an exception to the humble rule. This is during the "validation" phase of a sales conversation when talking about our skills, knowledge, ability, and experience becomes relevant and important. Here we can "brag" if we brag humbly and provide good facts to back up our claims.

Continue with Patience and Listening

Ego control and humility take our focus off of us. Patience and listening are tools that put our focus on other people.

Patience is important because people don't often know *exactly* what they want and *exactly* how to get it. If that were the case, there would be many fewer sales professionals in the world and a whole bunch more people who simply take orders. To sell effectively, we need to understand people's problems and understand these problems the same way they do. This takes time and listening and patience. Sometimes it takes a whole lot of these three things! This is part of selling and part of how we get people to say "yes" to us.

Dr. Scott Williams of Wright State University has a definition of "effective listening" that I like:

> "Effective listening is actively absorbing the information given to you by a speaker, showing that you are listening and interested, and providing feedback to the speaker so that he or she knows the message was received. . . . Effective listeners show speakers that they have been heard and understood."[1]

We can get conversations started by asking open-ended questions. These are how-what-where-who-why questions that can't be answered with a "yes" or a "no." Our body language and expression are important. We should sit straight and project interest and attention. We should "paraphrase" what the other person says— that is, put what we hear in our own words to confirm we have understood correctly. If the person expresses an emotion, ideally we reflect that emotion back to them. "I'm really ready to solve this problem," our customer might say. "We're ready to help you solve it," we should reply.

Patience and effective listening give us two valuable advantages. The first is an understanding of the problem that people will embrace. "Yes, that's exactly the problem I have," they should say. Great. Now we can craft a solution they will embrace as well. Second, patience and listening create a relationship of trust. Our buyers trust us because we've taken the time to understand their problem, rather than trying to sell them whatever it is we have. The relationship becomes a partnership. The conversation becomes a collaboration.

Finish with Collaboration

A collaboration is two people working toward the same goal for their mutual benefit. Once we have that—once we've built trust and we're working on the same side as our customers—then good things happen. People tell us what we need to do to earn a "yes." We are building solutions with people not for people, which means we are winning their approval all throughout the process. Little problems stay little because of the relationship. People keep coming back to us because they see us as part of their team, someone who is invested in their success as much as they are.

To Sell, We Must Be Great at What We Do

The second key selling skill is being great at what we do. We have to sell ourselves to succeed in today's world. This is absolutely true. The need for excellence in selling does not replace the need to be excellent in our work, however. Selling has become another skill everyone must have. If we can sell what we do, but we aren't good at it, we're still sunk. We're just sunk in a different way.

There is a higher level of excellence in our work, which is seeing creative ways to help other people. In the business world, this skill is often called "acumen," which I think of as the marriage of knowledge and know-how. When we have a deep understanding of our profession combined with the practical skills to deliver good results in the real world, then we have business acumen.

For instance, I have a friend in marketing with plenty of practical skills. He can create websites, email, and web ads campaigns. He can blog and tweet. He also understands the whole metabolism of how companies earn revenue—the interactions among a company's goals and people and products and services and customers, and how marketing fits into these interactions. My friend delivers results. He also can deliver new and different ideas that benefit everyone. They benefit the client because these ideas build the business. They benefit my friend because he gets more work.

Think about Mike from the flat screen TV story. His acumen was knowing that if I cared about the lighting in my kitchen, I probably care about the lighting on my television. He could see the problem with the television being on. And he knew how to fix it.

Acumen comes from experience. It also comes when we are curious, ask the right questions, have patience, and listen well. This works everywhere. Our goal is to find more new opportunities to help people and so find new opportunities to sell ourselves. The more opportunities we find, the more we succeed.

Take Your Next Steps Now!

1. Choose a professional relationship you want to improve. Use ego control, humility, patience, listening, and collaboration to do it.

2. Make the goal of this relationship finding a new idea—using your acumen—that will help the other person.

NOTES

1. From a *LeaderLetter* written by Dr. Scott Williams, Department of Management, Raj Soin College of Business, Wright State University, Dayton, Ohio. Dr. Wright uses these letters as a supplement to his Managing People in Organizations class.

9

Learning Is Selling.
Educating Is Selling.

I have learned a great deal from listening carefully.
—Ernest Hemingway

earning the needs and desires of our "buyers" is an essential sales skill. Many of our discussions have said that implicitly. Let me emphasize this "learning" explicitly before we get to the work of educating our "buyers" about us.

We've discussed reasons why confidence and humility are important. Here is one more: We need confidence and humility when we are educating ourselves. We're humble. We don't know all the answers and we need the other person to tell us. We're confident. It's natural for us to ask questions, and asking them is not a sign of weakness or lack of ability. Asking them is a sign of strength and expertise. Asking the right questions sells as well as having the right answers. Honestly, I think asking the right questions can sell *better* than having the right answers.

Educating ourselves about the wants and needs of our customers builds trust and relationships, which we know are important. There's one more valuable benefit to learning about our buyers. And it is:

Discovering a new need we didn't know—
and the other person didn't know—she had!

This is one of the most beautiful things that happens when we sell the right way. It is one of my favorite reasons why we should stop being Sales Apologists. This is one of the most satisfying things we can do in our lives. And it is one of the reasons I firmly believe—because I've seen it work over and over—that selling the right way brings us *more* success.

People who are just trying to sell what they have in their bag to whomever they meet will never experience this, because they don't take the time to ask the right questions and people probably don't trust them enough to answer the questions anyhow. Our next opportunity, even a bigger opportunity, comes from just such moments. When they come, the person is 80% sold already because we have their trust, we have the relationship, and we have the power of being the person who came up with the idea. That sounds good because it is good!

Educating Is Selling— for a Whole Bunch of Reasons

Sy Syms usually gets the credit for writing the slogan his company used: "An Educated Consumer is our Best Customer." Sy used the slogan to sell high-end clothing brands at great prices. We can use the same idea to sell our high-end brand: us.

Educating people is the multivitamin of selling. It has so many benefits, I hardly know where to begin. I'll start with one of my favorites.

Educating Shows Confidence

Educating people shows we are confident about are work. Educating says, "We want you to *really* understand what we do and how we do it, because when you do, we're confident you are going to choose us over everyone else."

That's powerful. When we give people with a "yes" we want the tools to make the best buying decisions, it makes us stand out. It also reinforces that we are committed to helping them find the best choices for their needs and desires, not just getting what we want for ourselves.

Educating Tells Us We Are on the Right Track

In selling, it is hard to know how serious someone is about saying "yes." Will this deal really close? Will this business really make a contribution? How can we tell?

Offering to educate people is an excellent way to test their interest. Let us come to your office and explain the benefits in more detail. Let us take you to lunch and answer your questions. When people say "yes" to these offers, it tells us they are serious.

How they respond to what we say tells us more. Do they seem excited or satisfied or intrigued? Most of all, are they asking *us* questions? Because if they are, that means they are interested. Always view questions from "buyers" as good signs and as invitations to educate and sell. Always see conversations as signs a sale can succeed. Because that's what they are.

Educating Removes Doubts and Answers
Objections before They Are Raised

It is natural and reasonable for smart business people to be benevolent skeptics. Good business people doubt nicely and in good faith. Doubt is not an insult or an accusation. Doubt is due diligence. Doubt is healthy and we should respect it because, when we are buyers, we doubt in good faith, too!

Educating is about removing those doubts. Some doubts may be doubts about us: Educating people is one more way we build relationships and trust. Other doubts might be about what we do: our skills, knowledge, experience, and ability. Doubt usually comes from not having enough information to make a decision with confidence. Doubt—if you like—is the parent of hesitation.

Educating people removes doubt and moves them toward a decision. Here is a simple example. Pretend we are the manager of a coffee shop and we are speaking to the owner.

> **Us:** I think we should replace our credit card machine and cash register with these little devices you attach to a tablet computer.
>
> **The owner:** Do they really work?
>
> **Us:** I set up a test account for us. Here, buy this scone.
>
> [The owner takes the scone, swipes her card, and touches the tablet to confirm.]
>
> **The owner:** Okay, you have my attention. Tell me more.

Us: You can see these are really simple to use. Our staff and customers both like them and think they are cool.

In this example, the "educating" was one step in the sales conversation. We introduced a new idea to the owner through a demonstration, and earned the right to tell her more.

A big part of sales is answering objections before buyers raise them. If people hesitate when they do not have enough information to make a decision, people offer objections when they have reasons to say "no" rather than "yes." Let's continue with the coffee shop.

The owner: I agree these little credit card devices are cool. But do they make business sense? Are they secure?

Us: The company has a good reputation for security. More than 5 million businesses are using the technology, and I haven't found news reports of problems when I searched the internet. Several other shops in the neighborhood use them and tell me they like them. The processing fees are the same as we pay now. We can record cash transactions, too, and the program will sync with our accounting program, which will save us time and reduce errors.

The owner: Okay, let's talk about how we make this happen. Good job.

In selling, we want to know what objections buyers will offer and have good answers ready. Objections are one way benevolent skeptics are skeptical. Objections are "obstacles" in the sales conversation that stand between us and our "yes." By anticipating objections, and preparing persuasive answers to them, we keep the conversations moving toward what we want. Even better, it increases our authority because it shows we deeply understand what we do. This understanding makes us look like experts, which is an excellent transition into—

Educating Clients Demonstrates Our Thought Leadership!

Thought leaders are often recognized national authorities, but we don't need to be a bestselling author or appear on television to show thought leadership in our work.

For example, if we teach grade school and know dozens of books that young boys really enjoy reading, then we can become the person other teachers ask when they need help choosing books for their students. Does that raise our profile in the school? Sure does. Does that make us more valuable to our "clients"—that is, our colleagues and the school administrators and the parents? Yes. We feel good about ourselves and good things follow.

The same holds true in an office or an organization or our neighborhood. When we educate people effectively, we become the person to ask. When more people ask us, we have more conversations. And what are conversations? Selling opportunities!

Educating Creates Realistic Expectations

One of the principles of selling the right way—so we never need to apologize—is that we don't promise more than we can deliver. Big promises make it easier for people to say "yes" to us. The problem is if we don't deliver what we promised, especially when we knew we didn't have the budget, time, resources, or opportunities we needed to deliver.

Are people happy then? Is the relationship stronger? Do they trust us more? Will they say "yes" to us ever again? The answer to all these questions is "no."

This is, of course, the reason why we under-promise and over-deliver. When we set realistic expectations, then over-deliver, people will become our life-long customers because we've proven we are honest, and we are effective, and we care about helping them as much as we care about helping ourselves.

Educating Makes Money from the "They Don't Know What They Don't Know"

Remember *The Epic Saga of Todd and the Flat Screen TV* from Chapter 2? Mike the electrician comes to my house to fix the lighting in my kitchen and does a great job. On the way out, he asks me if I have trouble seeing the picture on my flat screen television. He asks this because he knows the kind of lighting I had in the room with the TV often makes the picture difficult to see—and because he knew that people *don't know this.*

I didn't. I had tried all sorts of things trying to "fix" my television. My television was fine. The problem was the lights, and Mike took the time to educate me. Then he made a good proposal, I accepted it, he made more money, I was happier.

Mike made money from the fact that I didn't know what I didn't know about my lights and television. And by educating me, he discovered a new selling opportunity he didn't know existed when he walked through my door. It sounds like gravy or icing on the cake or manna from heaven. It's none of those things. What it really is . . . is educating!

Take Your Next Steps Now!

1. Think about a "sale" you want to make and the person to whom you want to make it. What are all the objections this person might use as reasons to say "no" to you? Write down how you will answer each of these objections.

2. Think about a topic where you can present yourself as an expert or thought leader. Write a short, entertaining, persuasive story that you can use to educate people about this topic.

10

Know How We Drive Results.
Show How We Drive Results.

*However beautiful the strategy, you should
occasionally look at the results.*
—Winston Churchill

O ur "results" are one of our most important sales tools. We often talk about results during the "validation phase" of the sales conversation, which is the moment when a person says to us:

"I like what you are proposing. Prove to me you are the best person to do it!"

This is a great moment because it means people are asking us to help them say "yes." We should take a moment to enjoy it. Then we reach into our mental research binders and produce our meticulously crafted, thoroughly digested, brief, clear, powerful answers that have facts, numbers, percentages, objective measures, recommendations, and reviews.

At the same time, we should remember that the "what" of our results becomes more memorable, and more persuasive, when we can tell great stories about "how" we got them.

Know "What" Our Results Are. Know "How" We Got Them.

I love facts. Facts don't lie. I love quantifiable results. They make sales conversations easier because good information makes it easier to make good decisions. We should feel great when we can say things like this:

> *"I helped increase sales 23% during the first year of my contract!"*

> *"I coached my daughter's soccer team from last place to winning the city championship!"*

> *"The changes I made reduced costs by 20% while increasing productivity by 12%!"*

> *"I organized my community to clean up our neighborhood park and won an award from the local Chamber of Commerce!"*

> *"My baking blog has 10,000 followers and gets 50,000 page views a month!"*

These are great results. How do we find great stories to tell about them? We go back to our old friends, our value propositions, for guidance. Our value propositions state the essence of what we do. They focus us on our key messages. And they help us build a bridge between *how* we got results and *what* those results are.

We can tell good stories by matching our value propositions with our results. Let's take that sales increase above and see how I would answer.

> *"I helped increase sales 23% during the first year of my contract."*

The person with the "yes" we want says, "Wonderful! How did you do it?"

> *"I did it by building Sales Culture. I showed how everyone counts, everyone matters, everyone helps make sales happen regardless of what their job is."*

Let's answer the question for the soccer team.

> *"I coached my daughter's soccer team from last place to winning the city championship!"*

"Wonderful! How did you do it?"

> *"My daughter's team didn't have superstars, but they all had guts and heart. So we practiced and practiced fundamentals and fought every second of every game."*

These sound good right? Persuasive, specific, brief, memorable. They tie our facts back to a story and emotions, and give them real punch. I love value propositions. I love them even more because value propositions help us when we find ourselves needing to solve this problem:

How Do We "Show Results" When We Don't Have "Facts" to Show?

We live in a world in which we can measure more and more things all the time. Yet there is still plenty of work where we can't show quantifiable, measurable results. What do we do?

The first thing we do is make sure our inner Sales Apologists don't get the upper hand and convince us what we do doesn't matter just because we can't put a number to it. Then we go back to the idea of telling stories that are memorable, show *how* we drive results in these stories, and most importantly tie the results to strong, positive emotions.

Let's talk again about Karen, who runs the cleaning machine at the printing plant. Karen can't show that keeping the plant clean increased sales by 17%. Karen can tell this story, however, and she does it using her value propositions as well as the principle of having a "direct line of sight to revenue" we talked about before:

> I do a good job cleaning the plant every night because I know a clean plant tells people we are proud of our company and we care about the work we do. It shows we are professionals committed to running our business the right way. It shows we respect and value the people who work for us. When potential customers tour our plant, they'll see they can trust us to do good work for them. And they are more likely to do business with us as a result. That's how I help our company succeed.

The non-profit executive we met in the Sales Apologist chapter can also use emotions to show how she drives results. Like many non-profits, her organization has a board that oversees all aspects of her work. On one occasion, a board member said to her: "You spend a lot of money meeting with donors. Are we getting good results from this money?" The executive answered like this:

> Yes, it is money well spent. I remember an event where I simply introduced myself to the man standing next to me. I didn't know who he was or what he did. As we talked, I saw he was interested in our work and realized his business had the resources to help us. So I developed a relationship with him. This took time and it did cost some money. After three years, we launched a campaign I knew he cared about and I approached him to make a donation. Not only did he say "yes"—he joined the board. You're sitting next to him right now.

Stories can be even more powerful than facts because facts impress the logical part of our brains while stories engage our emotions and inspire us to take action. The best stories contain hard numbers, too, but as you can tell from these examples, you can tell good stories that sell without them.

Selling Is Showing How We *Will* Drive Results, Too

Sometimes to make a sale, we need to show our buyers how we *will* drive results for them *now* in addition to showing our record of success in the past.

Let me tell you a story. During the golden age of IT, my friend Mitchell was a highly successful recruiter for a busy technology firm. His biggest challenges were that he could not hire enough engineers fast enough to meet the needs of his company or keep up with all the demands of his day-to-day work.

Mitchell lobbied his bosses to allow him to hire more recruiters, but they resisted because they saw the cost as an expense. Mitchell put together a strong business case for his request—showing how an investment in more recruiters would earn a good return in revenue and profits for the company by allowing it to grow more quickly. Mitchell's bosses agreed and when they saw the results, they pressed him to hire even more recruiters!

This is the classic "Return on Investment" model of selling, of course, and points out that a good plan for delivering good results is as persuasive as data on good results we've delivered.

Our Value Propositions Keep Us Focused on Delivering Results!

There's one more point I'd like to make. Not only do value propositions help us know how we drive results and show how we drive results, they also help keep us focused on continuing to drive them. James Anderson and his co-authors from the *Harvard Business Review* article said:

> *"Properly constructed, [value propositions] force companies to rigorously focus on what their offerings are really worth to customers."*1

Knowing how what we do matters helps us constantly—deliberately—consciously *keep doing it*. It keeps us from becoming complacent. We do something for a little while, we get good results, we become comfortable . . . and then our attention wanders. Just a bit. We're still fast, but become half a step less fast. We're still sharp, but become just a little less sharp. And maybe that doesn't seem like a big deal except that everything changes all the time these days. We don't have to lose much focus to miss something important. Then suddenly we discover we are behind on an important deal or trend or development or worse! On the other hand, if we use our value propositions to keep our eye on how we drive results, and showing how we drive results, we'll be happier and more successful people.

Take Your Next Steps Now!

1. Do you have three good stories with hard facts and numbers to tell about things you've done well? If you don't, prepare them now.

2. Is your success not easy to measure or quantify? Then prepare three stories that show you ***know how*** you drive results. Use the idea of "direct line of sight to revenue" to help you write them.

3. Do you remember your value propositions for what you do? Choose one and commit yourself to it by writing it someplace you'll see every day.

NOTES

1. "Customer Value Propositions in Business Markets" by James Anderson, James Narus, and Wouter van Rossum, published in the March 2006 issue of the *Harvard Business Review*.

11

Ask for What We Want. We Might Just Get It!

Ask for what you want and be prepared to get it.
—Maya Angelou

Let's consider where we are. We found our passion and our confidence. We polished our value propositions until they shone like fine silver. We built relationships, built trust, built understanding, educated, and always focused on the needs of the people who have the "yes" we want. We committed ourselves fully to their success. It's time.

It's time to ask for what *we* want.

What? You didn't think this day would ever come? Of course it was coming. The theme of this book is that selling is the common thread and the point of selling ourselves is to get what we need, want, and deserve.

The other theme of this book is "Now Stop Apologizing!" Those words are especially important here because the biggest problems our Sales Apologists cause happen when it's time to ask for what we want: when it's time to ask for the order or the new project or the new job or more money or the contribution or the referral; time to ask for help answering a question or solving a problem. We get here, and the Sales Apologists take over and we do what?

We don't ask.

Asking can be tough. I've seen excellent professional sales men and women stumble over asking for the "yes" when it was time. I've done it. The Sales Apologist in us gets the upper hand. The Sales Apologist in us whispers, "Maybe you don't deserve to get this, so don't ask." The Sales Apologist in us taps our shoulders and says, "Selling is not a good thing and if you ask for what you want, you'll be selling." The sabotaging Sales Apologist in us creeps up behind our back and hisses, "What if they say 'no'? Then what will *you* do?"

The most amazing thing about the fact "We don't ask" is how common not asking for the sale is—even among the most accomplished business professionals. Let me tell you a story from an old colleague, Bert.

The Business Development Team and the Question "Why Not?"

Bert was put in charge of the business development channel of his company, which helped organizations seamlessly implement large and complicated software updates. The software companies loved Bert's team because his team made it easy for them to sell more software more often. The organizations buying the software loved Bert's team because they made it easy to improve their systems without disrupting their work and losing time and money.

Part of the work of Bert's business development team was to be evangelists for their company's services and they did that well. A month or two after Bert arrived, he asked his team if they ever asked their software partners or their customers for a sale or a referral. They told him "We can't do that." Then Bert asked this question:

"Why not?"

They didn't have a good answer—except that maybe these good people, good at their jobs, all had bad cases of Sales Apologist-itis. Bert encouraged his team to start asking. He told them they had earned the right to ask because of the excellent work they did. When his team started, the company's revenue grew and so did their commissions. Even more importantly, Bert's team became more confident and they were happier in their work because they realized they *deserved* to ask.

You're Ready to Ask for What You Want

Everything we've talked about so far in this book has been about preparing you to ASK. Confidence and relationships and trust and listening and educating and committing ourselves to the other person's success—and most of all, not apologizing for selling—all give us the power to ask for what we want. They give us the right to ask because, like my colleague Bert said, we've **earned the right to ask**.

People understand that. People respect that. In fact, people respect us *more* when we ask for what we want because it reinforces everything we've told them about ourselves. People understand our interactions with them are about helping ourselves by helping them.

You know something else? When we sell the right way, people *want* us to ask them for what we want. They are waiting for us to ask. They *want* to say "yes" to us because we've earned that "yes." So what should we do?

Ask for What We Need, Want and Deserve!

Asking is the simplest and the hardest thing in the world to do. Here are a couple tips from a guy who spent a lot of years carrying a bag, knocking on doors, and asking for the order as a professional sales person.

One tip is that knowing when your "client" is ready to be asked for the "sale" is not easy. Here's how we do it. Think about the information and facts we have from the sales conversation. Do we think our buyer has enough information to make a decision? If the answer is "yes" then we check our instincts. Does our intuition, our gut feeling tell us *Now is the time*?

We're not always going to be right. Even the best sales professionals are wrong sometimes. We are not the buyer and we can't know what she is thinking and what she is feeling, or every factor and consideration that is going to affect her decision. We think hard. We check our instincts. Then we take our shot with passion and confidence and conviction. Let's be bold. There is power in asking for "yes"!

Tip number two is that we do know what we are thinking and feeling. When we can, let's ask for the sale on days when we are relaxed and confident and ready. There are some days when we are feeling great. Seize them and ask for the sale. There are other days when we don't feel quite right. On these days, avoid asking for that "yes" when we can.

We don't always have the luxury of choosing when we ask for the sale. If we have an appointment, we have to be up and ready for it. If the opportunity to ask takes us by surprise—and it's there and waiting—we have to seize that opportunity. This is one of the reasons that participating in sports and performing arts is excellent training for business. Because both ask us to perform our best at times and places we haven't necessarily chosen. It's great when we get everything just how we like it. Plenty of times in life, though, we work with the moment we have. That's why professional sale people work hard to be energized, focused, and positive all the time. That's because they never know when they are going to need to be!

My third tip is to ask for the sale in a relaxed and natural way. People often look for clues from us about how they should respond to our proposal. If we act as if saying "yes" is a big decision then our buyer might think it is a big decision, too, and hesitate. If we give clues that our offer is a good decision and there is no reason to wait, then the buyer might agree it is a good decision and say "yes."

These relaxed asks are also useful for "trial closings." Trial closings are a way for us to test how likely it is our buyers will say "yes" and how close they are to saying "yes" by asking for a sale before we really think our buyers are ready. Because we don't think our buyers are ready to be closed, we don't push too hard, we don't ask too directly. Our goal is to understand how much progress we've made in the sales conversation and to prepare our buyers to say "yes" to us later. We can do the same thing early in a sale to test if a buyer is a good prospect. Asking for a "yes" is a good way to test how serious a buyer is and see how much of our time we should give them.

Asking for the "yes" with comfortable words can also help. When a sale is a big decision for a client, I've found it is often more effective to say, "Are you ready to get started?" or "Can I place the order for you now?" rather than, "If we've got a deal, then whip out your checkbook!" In other situations, saying, "So what do you think? What would you like to do?" is better than the direct, "So what's your answer?"

One More Reason to Ask for What We Want

Finally, asking for a "yes" is a way to get a conversation that feels "stuck" unstuck. Sometimes this gets the sale and that's great. Other times, we get the conversation unstuck but this unsticking comes wrapped around the word "no" rather than the word "yes." This is not a bad outcome if the buyer's answer really is "no" because that can mean continuing the sales conversation is not a good use of your time or theirs.

The word "no" is interesting. It's not a word we love to hear like the word "yes" is. It's not the word that gets us what we want. The word "no" has authenticity, though. It has sincerity. It has truth. And it has strength because it is easier for most people to say "yes" than it is for them to say "no."

The most interesting thing about the word "no," however, is that it rarely means *"No. I will never be interested ever. I don't like you. Leave!"*

The Sales Apologists in us want to hear the word "no" that way. That's not what the word means. "No" is not where the conversation ends. "No" is where the fun begins! "No" is where the best things that happen to us in our lives often get started. In the next chapter, I'll tell you why and tell you how to take a "no" and make it a "yes."

Take Your Next Steps Now!

1. In the past, was there something you wanted and did not ask for? Why didn't you ask? How would you handle that situation differently today?

2. Is there something you want to ask for right now? If you haven't asked, why not? Have you done all you need to have earned the right to ask? If not, how are you going to earn that right? If you have earned the right to ask, how are you going to ask for it?

12

How to Make People Say "Yes" After They Say "No"

Say "no" to the good so you can say "yes" to the best.
—John C. Maxwell

ow do professional sales people see the word "no"? Do they see it as the person slamming the door in their face? Or do they see it as the person holding the door open and inviting them to walk through?

They see it as an open door, an invitation, and an opportunity. And so should we. This is more than my passion and confidence and optimism and persistence talking. There's science on it, too.

Daniel Newark and a team of researchers at Stanford found people believe when someone says "no" to them once they are likely to say "no" again. Participants in the study predicted that a person would say "yes" to a second request after saying "no" to a first request only 18% of the time.

In fact, 43% of people said "yes" the second time after saying "no" the first. "People consistently underestimate the chances [of hearing yes] after a previous refusal," according to Newark, and he found this to be true in several other studies he conducted.1

This means we should see the word "no" as an opportunity to win a "yes" by discovering why the answer was "no"—that is, an opportunity to listen to the person tells us what we need to do to sell them.

Let's seize it because our chances are pretty good we'll succeed!

The first step is to take the answer "no" in stride. In the last chapter, we talked about giving people "say yes to us" clues. We ask for a "yes" in a relaxed, confident way, and those are clues that our buyer should feel confident about saying "yes."

This works with the answer "no" as well except the clues we give here are even more important. We treat the "no" as a reasonable and natural next step in the conversation—not the end of the conversation. When we do that, people hear their "no" as just the next step in the conversation, too.

This approach also puts people who don't like to say "no" at ease. People don't like to say "no" because they don't want to offend us or upset us or seem confrontational or make us think they are unhelpful.

Finally, taking "no" well shows we are on our buyer's side. It shows we are committed to what's right for *them*; what will help *them* succeed. Selling the right way is about committing ourselves to the success of other people first. Our commitment is to what they want and need, not what we want and need. Hearing a "no" with confidence and grace and optimism and a strong desire to understand the reasons why shows we respect the other person. It shows we value our relationship with them more than we value getting any one particular "yes" from them. Taking "no" easy makes people comfortable and makes selling easier.

A Few Quick Tips on Our Next Steps after "No"

The first thing we need to do is acknowledge the person said "no." People want to be heard and to have what they say respected. So we should acknowledge their answer and do it fully and sincerely.

Then we ask questions to discover why the answer was "no." We should ask these questions in a natural and reasonable and easy way—just like we heard the answer "no." Because we've handled the "no" in the right way, people will be willing to answer our questions. We have also earned the right to ask the reasons why just like we earned the right to ask for the sale.

Ask open-ended questions that encourage the person to share details. Listen to the answers and don't argue with them. This is an excellent moment to use the simple technique of saying the word "and" instead of the word "but." The word "but" sounds like we are arguing and it stops conversations. When we use the word "and" we are agreeing with the other person, and respecting her, and finding ways to add to her ideas, and encouraging the conversation to continue. The word "and" is a great sales tool. Try it out and see!

This conversation, just like every conversation in the sales process, is a collaboration in which we are working with other people. We need to be humble and patient. And let's not offer a solution too soon, even if we have a great one, because that can feel like we are ignoring the other person's concerns.

These techniques work well in simple and complicated business conversations. Here is an example of a simple one:

Us [to our prospect]: Can we meet for coffee next week?

Prospect: I'm not certain. I'm not trying to be rude, I'm just not sure if it would be a good use of my time.

Us: I understand.1 If you don't mind me asking . . . would you tell me the reasons why?

1. *Take the "no" in stride and we will learn why our prospect said "no."*

2. *Here's our open-ended question.*

   Prospect: Honestly, I don't understand how this new technology works and I don't see how it can help my company.

3. *Information that will help us help our prospect.*

   Us: A lot of people say that. I have case studies other business owners have found helpful. I'd be happy to share them with you.

4. *Educating is selling.*

   Prospect: I appreciate that. I just wish this month wasn't so insane.

5. *Objection #1. Easy to deal with.*

   Us: I could call you after the first week of next month.

   Prospect: Yes, that would work. Can I be honest again? I don't know if I can get the budget from my bosses and I don't want to waste your time.

6. *Objection #2. Easy to deal with.*

   Us: I'm still happy to meet with you and help you understand the technology. Once you see how it works, I'm confident you'll see this is a good investment for your company and you will have a good ROI case to bring to your bosses.

7. *Focus is on the other person. Where it should be! Notice the word "confident." We are saying and feeling it here.*

Prospect: Okay, deal. Call me on the 5th.

8. *Bingo!*

   Notice everything in this conversation is selling the right way. Selling after we hear a "no" is basically the same as selling before we ask for a "yes." All we need to do is think differently about the word "no."

There are lots of reasons why people say "no" in business. Here is a catalog of some of the reasons I've seen. I've started with the toughest and worked my way toward the easier ones.

No Can Mean "I'm Not Comfortable"

Few people will say "I'm not comfortable" but we can hear it in their voice and see it in their body language. We can also tell they aren't comfortable when they answer our questions in awkward ways.

This is a common reason for saying "no" and it is often difficult to understand why the answer was "no." That's because people are telling us they don't *feel* right about saying "yes"—but may not be able to explain why.

This is a sign we have more work to do, and we need to pull out our listening skills and patience and get them ready. Remember the problem might be the person is not comfortable with *us* yet.

This "no" is also a sign that we likely asked for the sale too soon. Don't worry! Stay relaxed and confident and keep the conversation going.

No Can Mean "I Don't Understand"

This one is not as tough as "I'm not comfortable" because we know the problem. Our buyer doesn't have all the information he or she needs to make a good decision.

"I don't understand" usually indicates we've understood the problem, but we haven't done a good enough job explaining the value of our solution.

The good news is when someone tells us they don't understand, they want us to try again. They trust us. They are also telling us we could be the right choice for them, if we do a better job of educating them.

No Can Mean "It's Too Risky"

There is great news in this answer. We know we've earned our buyer's trust. We know she has enough information to make a decision. This answer tells us she was thinking about saying "yes" but something is tipping the balance to "no." What we want to know are the reasons why.

Often the word "risky" is a synonym for the word "new." So the problem might be we are asking our buyer to try something different. If we can make the new feel more familiar, we can make progress.

Another thing about the word "risk" is that people and organizations have different tolerances for it. In people, tolerance is driven by their personalities. In organizations, it's the culture. If we can understand the tolerance for risk in our buyer, we can adapt our offer accordingly.

Organizations that are large and old tend to be risk adverse. In these places, the way "we've always done things" carries less risk even when it isn't working. On the other hand, the rewards for trying something new that works well can be modest. So people in these places are often tough to sell.

No Can Mean "The Cost Is Too High"

Selling often involves money and sometimes the price is too high. This is good news just like "risky" is good news because we know we have interest, a match between our buyer and us, and trust.

Price can be an easier "no" to turn into a "yes" because prices are easy to understand. We offer one number. The buyer counters with another number. And so on. I'm assuming here that both sides are within the other's price range.

Finally, there are many times when a "no" on price is a bargaining tactic. Go after these hard because that means the "yes" is right there waiting to be seized. Just don't give away the store in the process.

No Today Can Mean "Yes Tomorrow"

This one is simple. Everything is good but the timing isn't right. The "no" was really a "not yet." Find out when the time will be right, and if there are factors that influence the timing. Then stay in touch, so when our buyer is ready to say "yes," we're standing right there to hear it.

Don't Forget at the End to Ask for Your "Yes" Again

At some point, the moment will come for us to ask for our "yes" again. Just like the first time we asked, we have to make sure we ask a second time. And a third. And as many times as are reasonable and appropriate in that sales conversation.

There are also times when "no" really is "no." The most successful sales professionals hear "no" all the time. It's natural. It's part of the game. But do you know what these professionals think when they hear "no"? They think the next person is going to say "yes"!

Take Your Next Steps Now!

1. The next time you ask for something you want, how will you prepare to hear the word "yes" and the word "no"?

2. What are three follow-up questions you could ask the next time someone says "no" to you? Write them down and have them ready the next time you ask for something you want.

3. Think about a time someone said the word "no" to you. How did you respond? How would you respond now?

NOTES

1. See "Need Someone's Help? Ask the Person Who Just Turned You Down" in an interview of Daniel Newark by Alison Beard in the December 2013 issue of the *Harvard Business Review*. Daniel A. Newark was a doctoral candidate in organization studies at Stanford University at the time of the interview.

13

We Are Always Selling. Especially When We Think We're Not

Luck is the residue of design.
—Branch Rickey

Every conversation, every interaction we have with everyone we meet every day, is a selling opportunity." I say that a lot. I said that a lot in my first book, too, because it is one of the core principles of Sales Culture. I'm saying it here again because the idea is just as relevant to selling ourselves as it is to selling for companies and organizations.

The idea that *everyone's in sales* means that everyone who touches customers is in sales, whether they know it or not, because how they treat customers influences the customers' decisions to say "yes." Everybody has an important role to play. Everyone's job is important. Businesses have lost big sales because of "little" things: the way their front-desk person greets visitors or the way a delivery person behaves. These same people have a tremendous positive impact when they do the same little "things" the right way. Everybody matters. Everybody counts. And we can matter and count without having to do anything differently. We just have to think differently about what we do.

These principles hold true when we are selling ourselves, with one small difference. Everything we *do* matters. Everything we *do* counts. We are always making impressions during "big" moments as well as "little" ones. Our actions matter in particular because our actions show we believe what we say, that our value propositions guide us. All we need to do is recognize that small moments matter and recognize that the key to selling in these moments successfully is to . . . relax a little.

How Do We Sell All the Time? By Not Always Making "Yes" Our Goal

There are many conversations in which it is not the right time to ask for something we want. There are many conversations in which it is not even clear that there is something for which we *can* ask. There is no sale for us in the conversation. We can still sell in it, however.

The goal of this kind of "selling" is to create good impressions, make connections, begin relationships, and learn something about the other person. We think about if there is an opportunity for us to help them or for them to help us later. Here is a humorous example of what not to do:

Person Working the Grill at a Neighborhood Barbecue: Hey, how are you?

Us: Great. I can save you 20% on your propane bill. Can I sign you up now?

That's the wrong way to sell every which wrong way there is in selling. There is still an opportunity for us here. We can be energetic and engaged and passionate and confident when we talk to people and they will remember that. Even better, we can be *interested* in them. We ask them questions about themselves and by doing this demonstrate an important selling quality, which is putting our focus on the other person.

Asking questions starts a conversation. In that conversation, we learn about the person and what they do. We are educating ourselves about them. Chances are good that once we've asked questions and listened to the answers, the other person will ask us questions in return. Then we could introduce what we do and our value proposition in a perfectly natural and appropriate way. Let's return to our cook-out example, because things like this really do happen.

> **Person Working the Grill at a Neighborhood Barbecue:** Thanks for listening to me talk for a while. So what do you do?
>
> **Us** [gesturing at the grill]: I sell propane although we sell to businesses not consumers. We deliver good service and help our customers control their energy costs.
>
> **Person Working the Grill:** You know, I buy a lot of gas for my restaurants and the price has been creeping up on me.
>
> **Us:** Do you want me to give you my card? I'll be happy to come speak to you and see if we can help.
>
> **Person Working the Grill:** Yes, let's do that.

Bingo! Make a connection. Start a conversation. Make a good impression. Listen. And discover new selling opportunities.

Inspiring, Motivating, and Influencing Are Selling, Too

Every sales conversation is founded on the fact our "buyer" is free to say "no" to us. All selling assumes the freedom of the other person to turn us down.

As a result, we might think that when we are in a position of authority—a leader, a supervisor, a manager, a coach—we do not need to sell. Leaders have the power to *tell* people what to do so they do not need to *sell* people on doing it.

The opposite is true, of course. Good leaders know that telling people what to do yields mediocre results. Good leaders get great results by making people *want* to do what the leader *wants* them to do. Effective managers sell by inspiring, motivating, and influencing. Let me give you a quick example of how a leader motivated and influenced one of his workers.

My friend Mitchell—the IT recruiter—began his career working for a rental car company. The supervisor of his location smoked in the office, back when it was legal to smoke in public businesses, but after it was considered unprofessional. One day, the regional manager made an unannounced visit. He smelled the smoke at the customer counter. He smelled the smoke more in the supervisor's office. The regional manager ran a large territory successfully and made a lot of revenue for the company. He had power. He could have handled the conversation many different ways. Here's how he did:

> **Regional Manager:** It really smells like smoke in here.
>
> **Supervisor**: Yes.
>
> **Regional Manager:** You can smell it at the counter, too.
>
> **Supervisor** Yes.

Regional Manager: I don't think we want our customers smelling smoke when they rent their cars.

Supervisor No, we don't.

Regional Manager: Do you know where the smoke is coming from?

Supervisor Yes. It's coming from me. I smoke in the office. I know I shouldn't, but I'm having a hard time quitting.

Regional Manager [looking at the ceiling]: Maybe the solution is we install a good fan up there in that corner.

Supervisor No, the solution is that I stop smoking in the office.

The regional manager knew the man knew the right thing to do was stop smoking, and he wanted the man to stop because he chose to stop—not because he was told. The regional manager could have given the man an order. Instead, he had a conversation. The regional manager could have lectured the supervisor. Instead, he treated him with consideration and respect. He influenced and motivated him.

Our executive at the disease non-profit could run her organization by telling the people who work there what to do. She prefers to lead with passion. She talks about why she's committed to the organization's mission. She attracts people who care about that mission and are inspired to do their work well because they care. "People don't buy what you do. They buy why you do it," says Simon Sinek in his leadership video we discussed in the Value Propositions chapter. Inspiring people may be the purest form of selling.

Solving Problems Is Selling, Too

Every sales conversation is also founded on the "buyer" having a problem the seller can solve. If the buyer does not have a problem, then we do not have a sales opportunity.

This means that every time we encounter a problem we can solve, it is a hidden sales opportunity for us because solving the problem gives us the benefits of having a "happy customer." Let me tell you a story.

My colleague Pete has a great job managing the integration of the IT systems of newly acquired companies with the IT systems of the businesses that acquired them. His goal is to help everyone quickly and efficiently and effectively adapt to the new systems as well as the culture and goals of the new company.

On one job in Europe, Pete was working with a large company that had gone through a lot of changes. They had recently emerged from a bankruptcy and they had been down-sized before they were acquired. The people in this company had survived a lot of changes before Pete appeared. During one meeting, when Pete was discussing the new organization of the IT departments, one of the European employees became angry, yelled at his boss, and stormed out the room.

Pete did not speak the man's language, so he didn't know what was happening. He was also more than a little nervous about the man's anger. The boss explained that the man realized the integration plans would eliminate his job. Pete said that was true, but there was a need for a similar job with skills similar to what the man would have. The boss tracked down the man (he'd made it all the way to the parking lot!), explained, and the man returned to the meeting, satisfied and happy.

Pete sees his work as selling. His buyers are the people who work in the acquired companies. His buyers are worried about how the changes in the IT systems will change their jobs and, in particular, if these changes will eliminate their jobs. Pete helps people say "**yes**" to the changes by showing them how they will benefit. If Pete were just concerned with IT engineering questions, he wouldn't be successful. And he wouldn't have built the trust and the relationships that are essential to doing his job well.

You'd Be Surprised Who You Meet . . . and Who These People Know!

Another reason every conversation is a selling opportunity is because we never know who the people we meet are or who these people know. We don't know who might be an opportunity for us . . . or us for them.

I have a friend who told me about the president of a business where he worked. This man was in charge of a successful, well-respected company, but he was not the world's best dresser. One famous story my friend swears is true—I kid you not—was that this president was nearly pulled off the street on his way to the office by social workers because of a "code blue" snow emergency. The president was brilliant at his job. He delivered good results. But he was occasionally mistaken for a homeless person who had to be protected from cold weather. If we were standing next to him in line at a coffee shop, we might not even say hello. And we would miss a chance to make a good connection who has good connections.

One more example. We all know someone to whom this happened. We are riding the elevator in an office tower on our way to a job interview. A person is riding with us.

Other person: Good morning.

Us: Good morning! How are you?

Other person: I'm fine. How are you?

Us: I'm very good, thank you. I'm looking forward to having a good day.

Scenario 2. Same people, same elevator:

Other person: Good evening.

Us [staring at our phone]: Grunt

You know what comes next. That person we greeted—or we grunted at—on the elevator? That's the person we are there to meet. The difference between the two first impressions we've made is huge. With Scenario 1, we walk into the interview and we've already established our energy and our passion and our confidence. We've already made a connection and demonstrated how we behave when no one who "matters" is watching us. With Scenario 2, we start in the hole even though we really are excited about the interview and confident we'll do well.

The "Crazy Luck" Some People Have Isn't Crazy Luck at All

We've all heard these "crazy luck" stories about someone who found their next deal, or their next job, or their realtor, or their dependable plumber—anything—because they struck up a conversation with the person next to them on a plane, at a game, at a bar, at a party.

These stories aren't crazy. And there is nothing "lucky" about them. These stories are the result of intention and consistency and practice and skill. These are stories about people making their own luck. This has been said a lot of ways. I like the way Branch Rickey said it.

Branch Rickey was the president and general manager of the Brooklyn Dodgers in the 1940s. It was Rickey who worked with Jackie Robinson to integrate major league baseball. Rickey said:

"Luck is the residue of design."

We don't know who people are, or who they know, and every time there is an opportunity to say hello, start a conversation, or make a connection, we should take it.

This doesn't mean that we should run around to random places and talk to random people. We should combine wide-eyed optimism with hard-nosed realism. We are always looking for the best places to find the best people who can help us. If we are looking to make sales in IT, we want to go where there are lots of IT people. If we want to become jazz musicians in New York City, we want to hang out in jazz clubs. This makes sense. We want to be smart about our choices.

At the same time, our lives are full of moments that aren't part of the "plan." Our lives are full of moments when we have the opportunity— if we take it—to make connections to the people standing next to us. The worst thing that can happen is they brush us off. Okay, no problem, no big deal. Lots of times we have a conversation for a few minutes. Sometimes, we meet someone interesting and helpful to us. So let's make starting conversations with people a habit. Many good things in life get started with a smile and the word *Hello*.

Take Your Next Steps Now!

1. The next time you get on an elevator with a stranger, how are you going to respond to them?

2. Look for opportunities to ask people "What do you do?" See what happens!

3. Identify a selling opportunity that doesn't look like a selling opportunity. (Think of Pete's story.) How are you going to sell in that opportunity now?

14

How to Get Other People to Sell for You— And Be Happy to Do It!

Alone we can do so little, together we can do so much.
— Helen Keller

No matter how hard we work, no matter how many conversations we begin, there are only so many people we can meet. We are all just one man or one woman, and the world is bigger than we are. We can only discover a fraction of the opportunities out there for us on our own.

That's why we need help. In my first book, *Everyone's in Sales*, I talked about the value of "relationship portability." Simply put, do we have relationships that will continue if we switch jobs or companies or industries or move to another city or country? Will people help us if we ask for their help? If people say "yes," then our relationships with them are "portable" and they are of immeasurable value to us.

The concept of "portable relationships" is important when we are selling ourselves, too, and it comes with a bonus. The total number of possible relationships we can make portable is **bigger**. That's because we can pull into our team family, friends, neighbors, and people we know from our communities in addition to all the people we know from our work. We can ask them to help us—and they will even be happy to help us before we ask—if we've built our relationships with them the right way.

People Will Be Happy to Sell for Us Because We Helped Them First!

"Selling the right way" is about long-term results. It's not about quick hits and quick scores. Selling the right way is a lot of effort. It takes time. We have to put other people's needs before our own needs. Yet selling the right way works. It gets us what we want, too.

Then selling the right way gets us more. All the time and work we did begin to pay steady dividends. That's because of a simple principle. When we help people, they want to help us. Not because we've earned that help, although we have. Not because they feel obligated to help us. They help because they *want* to help and because helping us makes them feel good. Helping us is a gift they give themselves. We don't have to apologize for this. Think about how we feel when *we* help someone we like.

The first way people can help us is by becoming part of our "virtual sales team." Within companies where we work, our virtual sales team is everyone who helps us solve a customer's problem or get a buyer to say "yes." Most of these people are not technically in the sales department, but as you know, *everyone's in sales.*

Selling for ourselves, we have our virtual teams, too. These are people who will help us by answering questions, or giving us feedback, or providing a resource, or making an introduction, or talking about their good experience with us. Our teams have things we need and are willing to give them to us. We are always "top of mind" with them. Our virtual sales team remembers us and what we do and what we want.

All we have to do is ask for their help. This means we give our inner Sales Apologists a good swift kick and then remember this:

People want us to ask them for help. So ask them!

Make sure people know specifically *how* to help us. Look at these two ways of asking for assistance with a job search we discussed in the Value Propositions chapter.

#1: "I need a better job that pays more money. Do you know anyone looking to hire people?"

#2: "I'm looking for a job as a sales manager in the medical technology, medical device, or pharmaceutical industries. Do you know anyone who could be a good introduction for me?"

The second one is much better because people know how to help us and they can do it easily.

There is an even more valuable way our personal teams help us. That's when they think of ways they can help us **before we even ask**. To do that effectively, they have to understand *what we do* and *why we do it well*. This means we need a quick detour back to our value propositions.

This Is Where Our Value Propositions Become Extraordinarily Important Again

In order for other people to sell for us effectively—to help us find good connections or introductions or opportunities—they have to be able to tell people what it is we do great.

They need to remember our smarts and passion and skill and confidence, too. It can be enough for people to say "She is a great musician—I've heard her play!" or "He's a great photographer—I've seen his pictures!" However, think about what happens when people can say things like this about us:

> *"She's a **musician** who can rock out at beach parties and play elegant classical music at formal events."*

> *"He's a **photographer** who can go to live events and take beautiful pictures that tell a story."*

We instinctively feel these are more powerful. Why? First, both provide details that sell the idea we are good. A musician who plays rock and classical music must be a great musician. A photographer whose photos are beautiful *and* tell stories must be a great photographer.

Second, both value propositions tell us about the opportunities that are good matches for our friends. A gala where there are younger people and older people is an excellent job for our musician. Public relations firms and event planners are super contacts for our photographer.

When people on our teams know our value propositions, they can help us more—which will give them satisfaction and make them want to help us again. Getting our value propositions right is hard work. See how it pays off, though.

People Will Sell for Us Only If We Keep the Relationship Fresh!

This isn't a criticism of the people in our lives. It's a simple fact. Everyone is busy. We're busy. Everyone has lots of commitments and concerns and obligations and relationships in their lives. We do, too. People like us. They want to help us. But it's easy for us to slip from their minds.

We need to keep our relationships fresh as a result. I'm old school and I still think nothing beats face-to-face meetings for coffee or breakfast, and if not face-to-face, then the telephone. Email is better than nothing, and for some people, it's the way they like to interact with us. Don't forget social media. It really is an effective way to have productive interactions with our virtual sales team.

Marketing people will tell you this is about staying "top of mind" with your network, and that's true. Remember, however, the best way to keep people selling for us is to keep selling for them!

And the Rest of the Selling Conversation Is Up to Us!

The members of our team sell for us the way our value propositions sell for us: by sparking interest, creating an emotional reaction, and starting a conversation. Then the rest is up to us . . . as it should be.

Our job is to thank our team member profusely . . . follow-up in a timely way with the contact . . . and inform our team member of the result and thank them profusely all over again *regardless of the result*. We do this, and they will sell for us again!

Take Your Next Steps Now!

1. Who are the people on your "team"? Do you stay in touch with them on a regular basis? If you don't, how will you start today?

2. Do you have a good friend you've lost touch with? Reach out to them and get the relationship going again.

3. Does your team know your value propositions? If not, how are you going to communicate your value propositions to them?

15

Are We Living in the "No" of the Past? Or the "Yes" of the Future?

There is nothing permanent except change.
—Heraclitus

There's one more important selling skill we need. It is the ability to answer this question: *Are we living in the past or living in the future?*

We often need to ask this question when we go after what we want. It is a question our Sales Apologist wants us to ask too soon—though it is a question we have to ask many times, sooner or later.

Most importantly, this is the biggest question we need to ask ourselves about our own lives, especially in today's world. Let me tell you one more story.

Once Upon a Time When "The World" Was My Oyster. Not My Customer

Back in 2007, I was a senior vice president of sales. Times were good. The company was making money. I was making money. I was hitting my goals. At the end of our fiscal year, my division managers called me into a meeting and said, "You've delivered great results. We are happy. You're fired."

I was puzzled. I was too surprised to have any other reaction at that moment.

"We would like to re-hire you in a great new position," they said. *Great!* I said and asked for details. "We'll talk about those later," they replied. I asked what this new position paid. "It's a good salary!" *And that good salary would be . . . ?* I asked. "We'll talk about that later," they replied.

I considered this information carefully. I weighed all the factors as they were presented, soberly and with deliberation. Then I said: "I would like the package, please."

After all, it was 2007. Times were good. There were jobs everywhere. I had a strong resume. What could go wrong? You know what went wrong. The year 2007 became the year 2008 and the bottom fell out. All those promising job leads I was pursuing? Bang. Gone. The sports-car engine roar of the economy was replaced by the sound of crickets chirping.

No problem, I thought. *The economy has been like this before. Companies may not want to hire new full-time, permanent employees right now, but they still need good sales professionals to help them.* So I reinvented myself as a "sales consultant" and discovered people get a look of desperate boredom in their eyes when you say you are a consultant. I then re-re-invented myself as a "sales coach" and discovered this was even worse.

I did find work in sales: a good contract with a good company. But that contract wasn't easy to get. From talking with my network, I did not hear the demand for sales consulting was growing. I thought about how people reacted to the words "sales consultant" and "sales coach." Then I said to myself:

"The world is your biggest customer, Todd. You better listen to what it says."

The most important sales conversation we ever have is between ourselves and the world. I listened to what my "customer" the world told me it wanted. The world was not saying "*I want sales consultants.*" The world was not saying "*I want sales coaches.*" The world was not showing me lots more opportunities for sales consultants and sales coaches. The world was certainly not telling me that jobs like the one I had in 2007 were about to appear again.

Was I happy about this? No. I liked the way the past had been. Was I scared? You bet. I saw clear signals that if I stayed living in the past, however, I was going to be in trouble.

I knew I had to do something new but I had no idea what that was. I decided I needed new value propositions, so I followed my value proposition steps. I made myself vulnerable and I had that conversation I've already told you about. I asked the man who'd hired me for the consulting contract what it was I really did for him and his company, and he told me:

"You've helped us build our Sales Culture."

There it was. Not fully formed, not complete and ready to take the world in thrall—but the foundation was there. There was a value proposition that I could sell *and* deliver. More importantly, there was a value proposition that understood the new world.

The problem with "sales consultant" and "sales coach" was that after 2008, everyone realized that just having an effective sales force was not enough to stay in business. *Everyone* had to be in sales for companies to survive. The principles of Sales Culture showed companies how to do this and make more money.

What I learned from my conversation with the world was that I needed to change. If I tried to live in the past—doing old things in old ways—I would keep hearing the word "no." I had to in live the future—and do new things in new ways—to hear the word "yes."

The Last Selling Skill We Need

Here's what selling is. We have a great product (us!). We know there are people that need what we do. We go out and we sell hard because we know there are buyers for us—people who will say "yes."

We don't know these people by sight. We have to talk to them. We have to go through sales conversations, and at the end, when we have talked to enough of the right people in the right ways, we'll get our sales and what we want.

Some people won't say "yes" and some conversations will not end in the word "yes." In fact, more sales conversations end in the word "no" than the word "yes." That's fine. That is a solid sign we are selling ourselves correctly. If we only talk to people likely to say "yes" to us, we will miss most of our opportunities and enjoy a fraction of our potential success!

Still, it is important for us to answer this question about each sales conversation we have:

Can We Still Hear the "Yes" We Want?

We've talked about how we need to combine wide-eyed optimism with hard-nosed realism in sales. In every conversation, we want to live in the future of "yes." When that "yes" is not there—in this moment, with this person, in this conversation—we move on. We learn from the sales conversation, tuck it into the past, and focus on our next opportunity.

It is difficult to know when a "yes" *really* is not there because few people will tell us "no" firmly and convincingly. When they do, our response is easy. We thank them and we ask for feedback we can use to sell ourselves better. Because we've sold the right way, and established good relationships, and asked for the feedback in a respectful way, people will be happy to talk to us. Don't let our Sales Apologists stop us from asking!

Remember, too, building relationships and trust are the two most important sales tasks. The person who said "no" to Offer A today may well say "yes" to Offer B tomorrow. This or that conversation may end up in the past. Relationships always live in the future!

It is not very often we get a firm and convincing "no," however. Instead, the conversation simply stops and we don't know **why**. It could be our buyer has decided to say "no" and doesn't want to tell us. There are a hundred other possible reasons, though. Maybe the buyer got busy. Something came up in his work or personal life more urgent than the problem we were discussing. Maybe the budget he needs to hire us has changed. Maybe his problem isn't quite big enough yet to make him want to solve it. Maybe his business conditions have changed. And so on.

Sales professionals rarely give up on a potential buyer because they just never know. They will carefully decide how much time and effort each potential sale should get. A buyer who is the longest of long shots is still worth sixty seconds every three months to telephone. Every once in a while, sales professionals catch a winner that way! We should do that too.

Did I make that sound easy? It is easy. All of selling is easy except hearing the word "no" especially when we've put work and thought and emotion into a sales conversation. It is hard to hear "no" when we've gone after something we really wanted and believed we could get. In the story I told you earlier in this chapter, it wasn't easy for me to hear the word "no." I didn't want to hear it, but I had to listen or else I would be still living in the "no" of my past rather than the "yes" of my future.

I work hard every day just like I did before. My world changed. I survived and then thrived, because I am a good speaker and good at selling myself.

You can do that, too—whatever it is you do. Sell yourself the right way. Don't apologize. Keep at it. And you will succeed. You will get what you need, want, and deserve. You will be happy.

So the time has come for the last of my *Take Your Next Steps Now!* questions:

How has *your* world changed? *and*
How are *you* going to sell yourself now?

You Are Ready to Sell Now

We need to sell ourselves because the world changed. Today, we must be good at our work AND good at selling ourselves to succeed. I know you are ready to get what you want because now you have all tools to do it!

Our first step was to defeat our Sales Apologists—those voices in our heads that want us to feel bad for selling. Then we learned to feel passion and confidence when we sell because these are the emotions that convince people to say "yes" to us.

We created powerful value propositions because value propositions are our key selling messages. Our value propositions tell people what we do and how we do it and most of all, why we do it. Our value propositions engage and intrigue. They start sales conversations. Most of all, our value propositions guide our actions. Our value propositions help us show through what we do what our values are.

We learned that the foundation of selling the right way is building relationships and trust. We know to do this by putting the success of our buyers before our own. We are patient and we listen.

We work with people as partners to understand their true needs. We give good information so people can make good buying decisions—including good information on the good results we deliver.

We learned how to ask for a "yes" because the whole purpose of selling the right way is to earn the right to ask for a sale. We know how to handle the word "no" and even more importantly, we know that the word "no" is the beginning of the fun in selling and not the end of it. We now see all the selling opportunities that surround us every day and how to seize them. We know to help other people help us sell ourselves.

Finally we are now living in the "yes" of the future. It is a great place to be. If I've done just one thing to help you live there, then I've achieved my goals for this book!

Todd Cohen

Todd Cohen, Principal of Sales Leader LLC and author of *Everyone's in Sales* and *Everyone's in Sales—Stop Apologizing. How to Get What You Need, Want and Deserve* is the nation's leading voice on building Sales Culture.

Todd is a dynamic, engaging and motivational keynote speaker and trainer whose message is relevant to every organization that wants to increase revenue, strengthen relationships and improve client satisfaction. Using humor and real-life examples, Todd demonstrates how everyone can contribute to the growth and profitability of the business. Todd shows how every conversation is a "selling moment" and this translates into personal and professional success.

Todd delivers approximately 100 programs per year to sales and non-sales persons around the world. Audiences range in size from small groups to upwards of 5,000 people. His clients are diverse. They include professional services firms, nonprofit organizations, closely-held businesses, national associations and global publicly-held corporations. Unlike traditional "sales coaches," who focus only on sales teams, Todd teaches the non-sales professional how everything he or she does impacts the client's and their colleague's decision-making process.

Todd is co-chair of the National Speakers Association (NSA) Sales Professional Education Group, a member of the NSA Chapter Leadership Council and the immediate past president of NSA's Philadelphia Chapter. He serves on the board of the Greater Philadelphia Senior Executives Group (GPSEG) and is chair of GPSEG's Sales and Marketing Group. Todd is also a member of the American Society of Training and Development. He served on the board of Pennsylvania Society of People and Strategy from 2011-2013.

Todd is a regular contributor to the *Philadelphia Business Journal*, has written for numerous trade and association magazines. Todd has published several whitepapers and monthly newsletter titled, Sales Culture Newsletter.

A dedicated networker and connecter of people Todd regularly works with people who are in career transition to teach them how to sell themselves and get the position they want. He served as the Sales Executive in Residence at Temple University Fox School of Business where he mentored students on entrepreneurship for 2010-2012.

Prior to launching Sales Leader LLC, Todd coached and led dozens of sales teams to deliver more than $850 million in revenue for leading companies including Xerox, Gartner Group, Thomson-Reuters and LexisNexis. Todd holds a Bachelors Degree in Business Administration from Temple University.

How to Hire Todd Cohen, the Sales Culture Leader for YOUR Organization

What is Sales Culture?

An inclusive environment in which everyone in the organization has a line of sight to revenue and impacts the client's decision to say "yes."

Teach your employees to think differently about what they already do and you've built a Sales Culture. Todd's services include:

- Inspirational and Motivational Keynote speaking

- Sales Culture Workshops™, Breakout Sessions, and Webinars

- Sales Culture Consulting—helping to create and grow your sales organization with a unique focus on the building the sales culture

To book Todd, he can be reached at
866-515-9445 or todd@toddcohen.com.

Book Todd Cohen for a Sales Culture Keynote or Interactive Workshop

KEYNOTE—"Everyone's in Sales"

This highly engaging and energetic keynote (and expanded workshop format) address is based on professional speaker and trainer Todd Cohen's book *Everyone's In Sales*. Todd's keynote is all about building a successful sales culture so more sales happen! A robust sales culture also ensures client retention and positive organizational engagement. Todd Cohen covers such areas as developing a professional value proposition, developing a virtual sales team and relationship portability. Todd will show each attendee how what they do contributes and how what they do impacts the customer and their ultimate decision to say "yes"! This is a timely and motivational message that speaks to the ability to create a mindset that everyone "sells" by doing what they do so well each and every day! Todd who relationship portability™ will also lead the audience through the building blocks of how to sell ourselves and motivate others to help us achieve our goals.

Session Objectives and Immediate Takeaways:
1. Learn the principles of a sales culture and conclusively know that what you do contributes to sales!
2. Understand and engage others with your Value Proposition
3. Definition of your Virtual (Sales) Team ™
4. Identifying and leveraging your Relationships Portability Index™
5. How to make sure that you are selling yourself the best possible way to get what you want!
6. Measuring Sales Culture ROI

WORKSHOP—"Networking Skills for the Successful Business Professional"

We all network every day! Is your networking paying off for you? Are you collecting business cards or making meaningful connections?

Networking is an essential activity for all business professionals and the modern day consulting professional is no exception. There is a vast difference between networking and networking in a way that builds consensus and support for you and your initiatives. Networking correctly builds business and drives revenue and profits!

In this highly interactive and fun session nationally recognized speaker and author Todd Cohen will take you through the 23 steps of networking and share how the best networkers make networking work for them! You will leave this session and immediately be a better networker and that skill set will help you get the return you deserve from your networking activity.

WORKSHOP—"Coaching, Not Telling"

A Workshop for Effective Coaching, Relationship Management and Accountability

"Everyone's in sales and everyone's a coach." Every conversation is a "coaching moment" therefore we are all coaching peers, friends, and family everyday. Coaching is a fine form of selling, and when you have the opportunity to help someone by coaching, do you respond by telling them what to do or by coaching them?

Being a good coach is a valuable skill and one we can all work on and be aware of so that we "coach and not tell!" The ability to influence and guide people to success is a paramount skill for positive outcomes, greater profitability and security.

WORKSHOP—"Creating Your Value Proposition"

This workshop guides each participant in the process of defining and validating their own personal selling statement or their value proposition. Knowing your value proposition ensures that colleagues and clients understand what you do and how you do it. That way your clients get served quicker because the right people with the correct skills are deployed every time!

WORKSHOP—"Build Your Virtual Sales Team"

This workshop guides each participant in the process of understanding and creating their own virtual sales team. The virtual team is a key component of building a sales culture and knowing why and when to turn to colleague and your community to be advocates for you, your company and all sales activity. The three stages of the virtual team are introduced and taught to be immediately leveraged.

WORKSHOP—Relationship Portability™

Your ability to recapture, renew and develop relationships can make a huge difference in how successful you are in being an active part of the sales conversation and hence part of the sales culture! Relationship Portability™ describes and instructs on how we can learn to keep our relationships portable, active and active as part of our virtual teams. The four categories of relationship portability are introduced and taught to be immediately leveraged.

WORKSHOP—"Presentation and Speaking Skills Training"

This session will cover the basics of effective presentation skills and how best to prepare for a presentation on your ideas and proposed concepts. Every day brings us the opportunity to present like a pro and the ability to present effectively and persuasively means we are selling ourselves and getting what we need to the best at what we do!

WORKSHOP—"Managing UP and ACROSS the Enterprise"

Managing and selling ourselves across our companies is an essential skill for all professionals at all levels. The session will cover the skills of how successful professionals manage the conversation and communications up and across an enterprise for a successful outcome for all parties involved.

WORKSHOP—"Objection Handling and Overcoming Obstacles"

Everyone faces obstacles every day and this workshop teaches how to handle common and unexpected objections and move the sales forward. Handling objections and overcoming obstacles is actually easy if we know the reasons why we encounter them and how to handle them in a systematic and fact based way.

Contact Todd at todd@toddcohen.com to talk about how he can customize a presentation or training session for you.

For volume sales of Todd's books, contact him at todd@toddcohen.com or 866-515-9445.

Visit Todd's Blog http://www.toddcohen.com/blog/